HERD

The Animals That Gave Rise to Humanity and Why We Need Them More Than Ever

HOBBS MAGARET

For Susana, Ever, and Vega

Orpheus taught while he sat and played the lyre, and his singing was so powerful that he mastered all nature. When he sang to his lyre, the birds flew about him; the fish left the water and sprang to him. The wind and the sea became still; the rivers flowed upwards to him. It did not snow, and there was no hail. Trees, and the very stones, followed after Orpheus. The tiger and the lion lay down near him, next to the sheep, and the wolves next to the stag and the roe.

Now, what does this mean? It surely means that, through a divine insight into the meaning of natural events, nature's happenings become harmoniously ordered from within. Everything becomes light, and all creatures are appeased when the mediator, in the act of worshipping, represents the light of Nature.

— **Linda Fierz-David**, *Women's Dionysian Initiation: The Villa of Mysteries in Pompeii*

FOREWORD

It's rare that a book challenges the way you see not only land and livestock but also your place within both. *HERD* does that. It offers more than a philosophy of grazing, it proposes a new operating system for thinking, managing, and living. As someone who has spent a career working at the intersection of grazingland science and producer-driven innovation, I can tell you that this book is not just timely, it's necessary. It's necessary because it challenges us to think differently about how we perceive the big picture. Challenging our own perception is healthy.

What strikes me most about the author is not just his intellect, but his willingness to let go of convention when it no longer serves the land. That takes humility, vision, and the kind of honesty that doesn't come from reading a textbook. It comes from living it, from putting boots on the ground and sweat in the soil. In this way, *HERD* is both a memoir and strategy to consider. It's a personal journey, yes, but more importantly, it's an invitation for the rest of us to challenge our perceptions about grazing, land, and life.

For too long, grazing management has existed in a tension between production and ecology. Too often, we have a tendency to view our livestock as a commodity and land as an input. This book flips that lens, not just to be provocative, but to offer a paradigm more aligned with how natural systems function. It asks hard questions: What if cattle weren't tools to be optimized, but co-creators of ecological health? What if ranchers weren't just landowners, but active agents providing balance between soil, sun, water, and hooves?

These questions matter because our current models are being challenged. Declining soil function, increasing input costs, ecological fragmentation; these are symptoms of a system misaligned with its context. *HERD* does not dodge these realities; it meets them with clarity, precision, and hope. This book is not about going backward to some idyllic past. It's about challenging our thinking and advancing forward, guided not by nostalgia, but by the deeper rhythms that have governed grassland ecosystems since the age of megafauna.

Reading this book, I was reminded of something we often say in grazing circles: "Manage the process, not the parts." That's easy to say and hard to live, especially in a world that prioritizes short-term results over long-term resilience. But *HERD* gives us a potential strategy to consider. It re-centers grazing in its ecological context, showing how herds are not just consumers of forage, but drivers of energy flow, nutrient cycling, and landscape function. This is a thought exercise in high-level systems thinking packaged in prose that ranchers, ecologists, and philosophers alike can digest.

Personally, this book struck a chord. I grew up with the conviction that grazing done well can heal land, and it can. I've spent over two decades helping ranchers integrate grazing principles with real-world constraints; drought, debt, generational pressures, policy limitations. I've seen the heartbreak that comes from doing everything "right" and still watching the land decline. I've also seen the quiet triumph when someone finally aligns their management with the land's own operating system. That's what *HERD* is about. It reminds us that nature is not waiting to be managed; it is waiting to be understood.

Perhaps the most refreshing is that this book doesn't offer a new set of prescriptions. Instead, it offers principles, philosophical and ecological, that can be applied across contexts. Whether you run cattle in the High Plains, sheep in the Hill Country, or simply seek to steward a patch of land somewhere in between, this book gives you something more powerful than answers: it gives you better questions. It invites you into a mindset where observation trumps ideology and humility outperforms certainty.

In a time when ranchers are pressured to choose sides; regenerative vs. conventional, grass-fed vs. grain, data vs. intuition; *HERD* reminds us that nature doesn't take sides. It operates in wholeness. It is not interested in our categories or arguments. It is interested in balance. And if we're willing to rejoin that balance, not as engineers of outcomes, but as students of process, we might just find a new kind of abundance. One that nourishes not only our landscapes and livestock, but our lives.

So, read this book not with the aim of agreement, but with the courage to be challenged. Let it move you from knowing to noticing. That's where real insight lives.

And when you're finished, don't just put it on the shelf. Put your mind to work.

—Dr. Jeff Goodwin
Director, Texas A&M Center for Grazinglands and Ranch Management
College Station, TX
June 2025

PREFACE

I could have reached out and touched the mountains if I wanted. But I didn't need to. I was already them. They were already me. Everything was one thing. Not even one thing. Not even no thing. And whatever it was—or wasn't—was totally empty!

Totally gone!

Let me explain.

In late summer 2015, my girlfriend and I lived in a shipping warehouse in Sisters, Oregon. We called it The Blue Keep because of its weathered blue metal walls. For much of my 20s, I had been playing, recording, and teaching music in that industrial space on the outskirts of a sleepy Central Oregon town—far enough from neighbors to make all the noise we wanted, but close enough to town to grab a coffee whenever I needed.

I wanted to be a rich and famous guitar player. At least that's what I thought. The truth, I later discovered, was that I believed that to be the only way I would ever get a ranch. Like my hero, the late great Stevie Ray Vaughan, I loved to plug a Stratocaster into an old amp and play too loud and too late. A decade into this life, I thought I had found my path. Even though rock 'n' roll was dead, I figured I would find a way. While I did indeed find a "way," it came with a bang and a capital "W."

This particular August, I had been reading a book—*Three Pillars of Zen* by Philip Kapleau. This book sat well with me, and I devoured it. I began a daily sitting meditation practice and started toying around with some of the methods of Zen practice outlined in the book. One of these methods was sitting with the Koan "Mu" from *The Gateless Gate*—a collection of Zen sayings and moments collected by the Zen master, Mumon. In Zen, koans are paradoxical statements or questions meant to disrupt habitual thinking—what some traditions might describe as tools for spiritual insight. The best description I've heard is "depth charges." You drop them in and with time and a little luck, they go boom.

> *A monk asked Joshu in all earnestness: "Does a dog have Buddha Nature, or not?"*
>
> *Joshu replied, "Mu."*

The written instruction for "Mu" is to just sit with it. Don't think about it or wonder what it means. Just hang out with it. Sit and, maybe, bring it up now and again. Just let "Mu" do its work. Over a week or so, I hung out with "Mu," but it turns out that "Mu" was hanging out with me. Mu began to sink into me. Lifting a fork became mu. Playing the guitar. Rising from bed. Walking down the stairs. This strange little syllable was causing something to happen, but I could not say what for sure.

Then, without warning, the shift happened. I was in the middle of teaching a guitar lesson, talking with my student about Son House's blues classic, "Grinnin' In Your Face." The song (which I recommend hearing) refers to the undeniable reality that no matter what you do, people will talk about you behind your back – in many cases quite disparagingly.

"No one can talk about you," I said to my student, Gabriel. Gabe was a junior in high school with long brown hair and a mischievous smile. "People can only ever talk about their conception of you. The idea they create in their mind. There is no 'you' for them to talk about. It's like they're shooting an arrow at nothing."

And with that, it happened. What exactly *it* was, I can't say. Something came over me. Or burst out from inside me. What I would have previously considered "me" began to melt into everything I would have considered "not me."

I wondered, "Could it possibly be happening?"

Three Pillars of Zen contains a section where it outlines various awakening experiences of practitioners across the years, and the previous evening, I had read an account of a businessman on a train. It was a man named Yamada Koun, a Japanese businessman and long-time practitioner of Zen. His account reached a climax of his awakening in the middle of the night where he was startled from his sleep in the full throes of an awakening experience, what Zen calls a "kensho" or "seeing one's true nature." He jumped up and down and cried and laughed and yelled—a common experience in a deep awakening and a foreshadowing of what would shortly be descending upon me.

I looked at my student and, without any conscious

effort, I started laughing—a deep, unstoppable laughter, as if I were discovering joy for the very first time. Tears filled my eyes, and I felt an overwhelming surge of energy, rushing through me like a flood. In that moment, there was no separation between me and the world around me. In many spiritual traditions, laughter and tears often accompany moments of profound insight, and now I understood why.

"What's going on?" Gabriel asked.

Still laughing, I gently tapped him on the forehead and said, "It's real! It's happening! I can't teach you any more today. You can head out—this lesson's on the house."

After Gabriel left, the experience surged even further. Something fundamental had started to shift. The edges of what I thought of as "me" were cracking but somehow still holding together. I ran upstairs and told my girlfriend, "It's happening."

"What?" she asked.

"What the book talked about."

As fate would have it, my mother-in-law was staying with us for the weekend, and I knew she wouldn't understand what I was going through. Thankfully, she was out at the store, giving me just enough time to drive to my parents' house a few miles away.

As I left the industrial park and merged onto Highway 20, a flood overwhelmed me. Tears streamed down my face as I sobbed uncontrollably—not from sadness, but from a profound, awe-filled release that defied explanation. Everything I had thought about myself and the world seemed to dissolve in that moment.

Leaving Sisters and heading east, I could see the Three Sisters mountains to my right, standing majestically, shining as the afternoon sun began to find its evening warmth. But the mountains were not mountains. They were me. And what's more: they were totally and completely gone. It was there, but it was absolutely gone. Vanished. The whole world. The whole universe—one great unavoidable emptiness.

In my wailing and sobbing, I cried out. "Oh my God!! It's true!! They weren't lying!!" (Apparently another common reaction.) Tears streamed down my face as everything I thought I knew, everything I thought I was, and every thought I had ever had about anything became null and void. The illusion of separateness had completely shattered.

The gravel crunched under my tires as I pulled up to my parents' house, nestled at the edge of the Deschutes National Forest. The familiar sound of their dog, Smokey, barking sharply at the door greeted me as I approached. My mother answered, her eyes immediately locking onto mine. She could tell something profound had happened.

"What's wrong?" she asked.

"It's real!"

I sat on the patio on the back porch of my parents' house, looking out at the mountains. It was as if I could reach out my hand and touch them. But why would I even want to? They were already me! There are no mountains, and there is no me. And what's more, it's all just one great emptiness. And it's all one! It's all the same thing! And it's nothing at all! There is no connection! How could anything ever be connected to anything else? It's all just ONE!

Standing up, sitting down. Laughing. Crying. Talking. Not talking. All the same. All one. All empty.

And more beautiful than anything I could have ever imagined.

I was changed. Forever.

After some time, the "experience" receded enough that I was able to return home. My parents drove me and dropped me off at The Blue Keep. That night, I didn't sleep. In the morning, I could do nothing but sit on my meditation cushion and cry.

I soon connected with Zen teacher Henry Shukman, who, after hearing my story, recognized the experience for what it was—an awakening well-documented in the centuries-old Zen tradition. His guidance helped me begin to integrate this profound shift into my everyday life.

But life didn't make the transition easy. Over the next two years, everything I had built seemed to crumble—my business failed, my band dissolved, and my wife and I faced eviction. We had a newborn on the way and no clear plan. It felt as though the old world had to fall apart for something new to emerge.

But I still had that great gift. A gift more valuable than anything on Earth. I knew that everything was one. I KNEW it. And I KNEW that everything is one great beautiful gymnastic emptiness. I knew it in the way, as some Zen people say, that you know your own father in a crowd. You need no one else's confirmation.

And I knew then, as I know now, the great gift of that moment—of that experience—was this very moment right now. All bets were off. Anything was possible, because it was all one. All empty. All me.

The Buddha declared, *"Throughout heaven and earth, I alone am the Honored One."* Jesus echoed this truth when he said, *"The kingdom of God is in your midst."* Though I stumbled upon this understanding through Zen, I have since realized that it resonates across cultures and traditions. The desert mystics, indigenous naturalists, and Romantic poets have all hinted at the same profound inseparability of self and world. Even Jimi Hendrix, in his own way, might have been pointing to this truth when he sang, *"I stand up next to a mountain and chop it down with the edge of my hand."*

I finally knew what they were talking about, but what now?

One very difficult year later, I was sitting at the kitchen bar in my in-laws' house in Los Angeles as my (now) wife and I were getting our lives together. No easy task with no money and a newborn. I had spent the previous six months trying desperately to create some kind of momentum with music in Los Angeles, but to no avail. My heart just wasn't in it. There was no blood in the music. Only water.

I was lost, struggling to find a sense of purpose in the world after everything had fallen apart. Desperation crept in, and I hit rock bottom. But sometimes, it takes deep darkness to notice the faintest light. That light was the enduring legacy of my family's ranching heritage—a connection that had quietly sustained me through everything.

My family had been ranching in the Texas Panhandle since the late 1800s. Generations of us worked the land—my great-great-grandfather managed a division of the legendary XIT Ranch, and nearly all my forebears carried on that tradition. I was born into it, spending my earliest years on horseback and around cattle.

One of my earliest memories is riding in the truck with my grandfather across the Pacheco Ranch near Clayton, New Mexico, when he suddenly stopped. In the fading sunlight, he had spotted a coyote—a faint gray shape blending perfectly into the landscape—hundreds of yards away. He reached for his old .22-250, always within arm's reach on the floorboard by his leg. He steadied the rifle on the side mirror, aimed, fired, and the coyote dropped.

"Got 'em," he said.

It's worth mentioning that I don't advocate for indiscriminately killing coyotes. Like many ranchers of his generation, my grandfather saw them as threats and acted according to the norms of the time. But what stood out to me wasn't the shot itself. It was the fact that he saw the coyote in the first place. He was so deeply united with the land, he couldn't help but see what most people would never have noticed.

I had spent years trying to run away from ranching, but it had finally reeled me back in. As my grandfather often said, "There's no retirement in ranching." I began applying and interviewing with ranches across the country—large and small, progressive and traditional. Each operation had its own approach, shaped by different philosophies and methods. Some drew inspiration from the gurus of regenerative agriculture, each with their book, pamphlet, or TED Talk. So, I immersed myself in their ideas—reading Allan Savory, Jim Gerrish, Joel Salatin, Johann Zietsman, and many others. Each perspective offered valuable insights, but I struggled to find a system that fully aligned with the vision that was beginning to crystallize in my mind.

They were all useful and informative, but when I read Johann Zietsman's *Man, Cattle, and Veld,* I knew I had found the door I wanted to walk through. Zietsman had pioneered Ultra-High-Density grazing—a system that challenged conventional ranching wisdom by embracing the natural dynamics of grazing animals and ecosystems. His approach resonated deeply with me, not just for its practicality but for the way it seemed to align with a broader truth: the unity of all creation. He saw through many of the inefficiencies and misunderstandings that plagued traditional ranching practices and offered a way forward rooted in both observation and ecological harmony.

At the time, Ultra-High-Density grazing was still a relatively new and niche approach, with few opportunities to find work in established operations. My wife and I made the decision to return to Oregon and start our own grazing operation. We scraped together enough money to get started, and with the support of some incredible friends and family (and a fair amount of luck), we were off and running. The early years were filled with trial and error, but every challenge taught us something new. Slowly but surely, we began to find our footing, and we haven't looked back since.

I would like to emphasize that this experience was not an indication of having accomplished anything. It was simply a gift. Perhaps the greatest gift of my life, but a gift nonetheless. This book isn't intended to be about Zen, religion, or mystical thought per se, though those influences have shaped my perspective. Instead, it's an effort to articulate an understanding that is still arising from experiencing the world as one indivisible whole. It's about recognizing that there is no separation between land, animals, and people—everything operates as a singular, dynamic reality. The challenge lies not in conceptualizing this truth but in discovering how to live and act from that place of inseparability.

Science has made intriguing progress in recent years, revealing that the universe functions in ways that challenge our everyday assumptions about time, space, and causality. While reality may not always conform to simple cause and effect, the world presents itself in that form, and that's how we interact with it.

This book explores how recognizing the inseparability of all life can serve as a foundation for ecological and ranching principles. By harnessing the natural patterns and rhythms of the land, animals, and ecosystems, we can create positive, self-reinforcing cycles that benefit both the environment and those who depend on it. Grazing, nature, humanity, and civilization are not separate entities but expressions of a unified whole.

Many of the problems, distortions, and negative consequences in the world today are rooted in the illusion of separation. The assumption that humans, animals, and the land exist as distinct and independent entities leads to actions that degrade both ecosystems and societies. While the full realization of inseparability may not be universal, we can and must create safeguards to prevent the harm caused by this illusion. Recognizing this unity is not just a philosophical stance—it is essential for cultivating resilience and harmony in both ecological and human systems.

We can't all retreat to a desert or mountain top for a life of introspection—and truthfully, few of us would want to. Life demands that we engage with its daily realities: paying bills, caring for others, and doing the work at hand. Yet, in navigating these responsibilities, we often lose sight of the inseparability beneath it all. Many people live their entire lives rooted in the illusion of separateness, unaware that another way of seeing and being is always within reach.

Separateness and oneness are two faces of the same coin. We can look at either side of this beautiful coin, but we can't spend just one. Both perspectives are present in every moment, whether we realize it or not.

Words can never capture the full flavor of that experience—only a taste—but this writing springs from that pivotal moment in late summer 2015. In some strange way, my ranching career has mirrored that awakening. I returned to the same world I had always known, yet everything had changed. The animals, the land, and my role within it all shone in a new light.

I was born a rancher and reborn as a naturalist. Maybe one day—if I'm lucky—I'll just be a rancher again.

—Hobbs Magaret

TABLE OF CONTENTS

INTRODUCTION

"Is that not what a bull is supposed to do — jump?"

– Johann Zietsman

Wilbur and Orville Wright created the first functional airplane, but they were not the only ones trying. Scores of well-paid, academically trained engineers were employed by big corporations to solve this problem as well. So how did a couple of bike mechanics from Ohio solve the problem before the trained engineers? They looked to nature.

Where others sought to overpower air currents with brute force, the Wright brothers turned their eyes to the sky and observed how birds navigated the wind with effortless grace. Instead of defying the air, the birds danced with it, their movements a living partnership with the elements. Inspired by this perfect natural design, the Wrights crafted a plane that could collaborate with the currents instead of fighting them—and they changed the world.

The lesson here is simple but profound: those who work *with* nature, rather than attempting to dominate it, unlock extraordinary potential. This principle applies to agriculture just as much as aviation. Like the Wright brothers, those of us who care for the land can only succeed when we abandon the impulse to impose control and instead learn to partner with nature's rhythms.

Inspired by nature's perfect design, Wilbur and Orville Wright successfully flew the Wright Flyer in December 1903 and changed the course of history.

Today, cattle raising is largely driven by a mindset of control and optimization, where engineers and academics design systems to force productivity and fertility. The result is an endless barrage of fossil energy inputs—supplements, vaccines, minerals, vitamins, probiotics, and more. This mechanistic approach, while efficient in some respects, has overshadowed the subtle wisdom of nature's own processes. The elegance of ecological balance has been supplanted by cold, calculated industrialism, often at the cost of long-term sustainability.

Today, a few visionaries are breaking free from the programming of industrial agriculture. By releasing their need to dominate and manipulate, they allow the land to guide them. In doing so, they discover something unexpected: heightened awareness and minor superpowers—an uncanny sense of timing, perception, and intuition—emerge as natural outcomes of this partnership. They don't impose their will on the landscape—they move in harmony with its rhythms.

These individuals find themselves aligned with the practices and wisdom of cultures that have preserved their deep connections to the natural world. Minor superpowers, sharpened instincts, and an expanded perception become downstream effects of this partnership. The prizes of this connection are not new. They are timeless and often manifest in ways that challenge conventional logic. Consider the Aboriginal Australians and their Songlines...

If you happen to find yourself fortunate enough to be with a Native Australian deep in the Outback, you wouldn't point at a feature of the landscape, such as a mountain or desert, and ask, "What is that?" You would instead ask, "Who is that?" To these people, the land is not a "what." It is a "who," and these beings and their deeds are immortalized in Songlines. A songline is part song, part map, part property survey, part migration route, and part history. Yet, even those labels fail to fully capture its essence. My description will never be adequate. I am not an Indigenous Australian and cannot fully grasp the depth of this knowledge. But, if they will forgive me, I would like to share my understanding in the hopes of conveying even a glimpse of its beauty and significance.

You see, Indigenous Australians did not have territories with hard boundaries as you would think of a modern nation or property having. They had songlines. Any member of a group could travel their section of a songline, even if it crossed through another group's songline.

The custodians of these songlines not only knew the routes by heart but could also sing them. Each note, phrase, and theme represented a physical feature or event along the route. Though each custodian might only traverse one section in their lifetime, the songlines stretched across the entire continent, forming an interconnected map of knowledge. Remarkably, custodians knew the entirety of these vast routes by song—even if they had never seen every part of the journey. To use a modern analogy, it's as if you inherited a portion of a highway. You might never drive its full length, but you would still know the route from one coast to the other.

These songlines also conveyed the history of "The Dreamtime," a deeply significant Aboriginal understanding of the world's origins. In this tradition, the Dreamtime Ancestors shaped the physical world through their actions and journeys. Prominent features along a songline—mountains, rivers, or deserts—are often seen as sleeping ancestors, while the surrounding landscape bears the marks of their activities. Custodians of the songline knew these stories in full, even if they had never physically visited every place described within them.[1]

Perhaps most astonishingly, a person could hear a segment of a songline recorded at one end of the continent and immediately recognize and continue it, even if they lived thousands of miles away on a different section of the same songline. Despite vast geographical and linguistic differences, they would seamlessly adapt the melody and structure using their own words. How this is possible remains a mystery. Some theories suggest parallels with the magnetic navigation used by migratory birds. Personally, I wonder if it might also be an expression of a shared memory akin to Carl Jung's concept of the collective unconscious. The truth, however, eludes scientific explanation.

I should also mention that songlines are astonishingly long. Some span distances equivalent to the length of Homer's *The Iliad,* which contains over 12,000 lines. The

---

1. Bruce Chatwin, *The Songlines* (London: Jonathan Cape, 1987).

sheer volume of knowledge and memory required to carry these songs is, by any standard, mind-boggling.[2]

It's fair to say that the entire existence of pre-European Australians was built on a profound unity with Nature. They didn't see the land as a separate entity—it was alive, and they were a living extension of it. This inseparability shaped every part of their world, their stories, and their survival.

Some people today, particularly those deeply attuned to the natural world, have retained glimpses of this unity. Here's a short example of a minor superpower that can arise from such a connection:

Many great cattlemen and women have what can only be described as an uncanny sense for gathering pastures. When ranchers need to gather (or muster) a large pasture, the basic concept works like this: They spread out on one side and work like a net, driving the cattle across the landscape toward the desired destination. The problem is that many of these pastures are so vast they can't see each other for hours at a time. Yet, the best of these practitioners always seem to show up on the right hill or come out of the right valley at the perfect moment. They just know.

Some of us, me included, experience something even stranger: the sensation of literally feeling the magnetic field of a herd of cows or a horse. It's a subtle, almost imperceptible awareness—a tug in the air, a shift in presence—that defies logic but proves reliable in practice. Perhaps it's the result of generations spent working on the

---

2. Bill Bryson, *A Sunburned Country* (New York: Broadway Books, 2001).

land, an embodied connection to the rhythms of life that transcends conscious thought. I've often wondered if this is an epigenetic inheritance, a minor superpower shaped over at least six (at least) generations of my family living in close partnership with animals and landscapes.

The phenomenon is not limited to cattle. Many great horsemen and women experience something equally extraordinary with their horses. Or perhaps it's the horses that share the connection with us. My mother once told me a story from her time working for the hall of fame cutting horse trainer Pat Earnhart in Hernando, Mississippi. She was exercising the legendary cutting horse Peppy San, who was well into retirement at that point. While loping him in a circle, a thought flashed through her mind: "I'm going to close into a tighter circle." Before the thought had even fully passed, Peppy San had already done it.

These moments of deep unity may seem coincidental to outsiders, but for those who have spent thousands of hours on the land or with animals, they take on a different significance. They become markers of a partnership so profound that it challenges our assumptions about separation and control. There are countless stories of unexplainable phenomena in the natural world, and these are just a few of the ones that have stayed with me—stories of minor superpowers that arise from unity with nature.

You can't be on the land for any meaningful period of time without it changing your very DNA. It rewires you, attunes you to the landscape in ways that science has yet to fully understand.

Modernity has largely severed us from these connections.

In our pursuit of convenience and control, we have distanced ourselves from the vast, untapped possibilities that come from being in partnership with nature. The dominant paradigm of scientific materialism, which has elevated technology to the pinnacle of progress, has undeniably brought prosperity and comfort. Yet, it has also brought a profound disconnection—one that impoverishes both the landscape and the human experience by cutting us off from the underlying unity that sustains all life.

This fragmentation is perhaps most evident in agriculture. Land, animals, and people are treated as isolated components in a mechanized system designed for maximum output. Nature becomes little more than a set of chemical and mechanical processes, managed through domination rather than dialogue. While this industrial mindset has increased yields, it has also degraded the soil, eroded biodiversity, and weakened the resilience of entire ecosystems. Worse still, it has severed us from the deep, regenerative relationship that once defined our place on Earth.

But nature is not a machine. It is a living, dynamic symphony—a trillion interconnected forces engaged in a serious yet playful dance of becoming. Acknowledging this truth requires a cultural "depth charge"—a disruption of deeply embedded assumptions that blind us to nature's wisdom.

I hope that this book, in its exploration of ecological principles and humanity's place in them, can offer a small step toward that awakening.

I. HERDS
RETHINKING WHAT MATTERS

"The way the world makes itself manifest to us is in accordance with our aim, our attention, and our values."

- Jordan Peterson

I have spent thousands of hours searching for the root of agriculture's dysfunction. Our methods undeniably succeed at producing food, but they fail spectacularly when tasked with sustaining ecosystems over centuries. Civilizations have crumbled time and again over the last 5,000 years because we have never mastered the art of uniting culture and ecology into a truly self-replenishing process.[3]

After wading through mountains of books, papers, and conversations—both face-to-face and digital—I have come to an uncomfortable conclusion: agriculture, as we know it, was designed to fail. It collapses not in spite of our best efforts, but because of them.

We are hitting exactly where we've been aiming.

---

3. Chew Sing C. World Ecological Degradation: Accumulation, Urbanization, and Deforestation 3000 BC-AD 2000. Rowwman Altamira, 2001, p.1.

Our mental model of the world is flawed. To cultivate truly harmonious grazing and agricultural systems, we must first align our foundational understanding of the world—and our place within it—with reality. Without a solid conceptual foundation, we are doomed to repeat short-sighted, unsustainable practices.

Understanding complex systems is like starting a young horse: you don't just jump on and ride. You begin by pulling on your boots.

The Earth has an operating system—a user manual of sorts. Rule number one for managing landscapes at scale might read: Grass harvests sunlight, herbivores graze on grass, and predators manage herbivores. Ensure all components are present and functioning correctly.

The key word here is "correctly." As both protectors and predators of the natural world, we have clearly failed to maintain these systems. Any seasoned observer of our natural landscapes can see this truth plainly.

Throughout history, agriculture has occasionally fostered flourishing landscapes, though this is likely the exception rather than the rule. Today, however, large-scale industrial agriculture is supercharged in its capacity to degrade ecosystems. Driven by short-term thinking and fragmented principles, it accelerates atrophy, soil erosion, and species loss at an unprecedented scale. Yet, examples of regenerated, thriving landscapes remind us that alternative paths are possible if we realign with the deeper processes of nature.

The root of this ecological decline is largely a

consequence of a worldview that sees humanity as separate from nature. When we unconsciously operate from a sense of exile—believing that we are apart from the Earth rather than a part of it—our actions lead to imbalance, despair, and collapse. We must remember: the ecology is not something outside of us. It is us.

Even if we intellectually grasp that humanity and nature are interwoven, our actions will still produce degradation unless we fundamentally shift how we orient ourselves to the biosphere. Understanding is not enough; it must translate into behavior. Because human motivations are often hidden—even from ourselves—our best defense lies in establishing principles that serve as both a compass and a safeguard against our shortsighted impulses.

A sound principle must be robust enough to support an entire worldview without fracturing under pressure. When principles are properly aligned with reality, each new idea or decision integrates harmoniously, preventing unforeseen consequences and distortions.

A weak foundation might hold three floors but will collapse under the weight of a fourth.

A strong philosophical foundation, however, is built on basic truths that do not contradict one another. From these truths, we can make decisions that align with the natural order. To navigate reality effectively, our actions must be grounded in principles that mirror the world's true workings.

Put simply: Build your house on the rock—not on the shifting sands of expediency.

So, what is the rock upon which we build our house? Let me state it plainly:

Herds exist to maintain and enhance ecosystem processes.

This is the key piece, and the rest of this book will explore this concept along with a few supporting ideas—most importantly, humanity's role in facilitating these processes. Together, these ideas offer the potential for a new kind of abundance—one that arises naturally from harmonious interaction, rather than being extracted from an unwilling and depleted ecology.

Humanity is notoriously short-sighted, often struggling to see beyond immediate needs and desires. The concept of long-term planning and deferred gratification is a relatively new development in our evolutionary history. Yet, with the responsibility of managing large-scale ecological processes now in our hands, we can no longer afford this narrow vision. To fulfill this role effectively, we must adopt a long-term perspective grounded in accurate, consistent, and repeatable principles.

To construct a coherent philosophy, we must begin by consolidating our core assumptions. Build the foundation first—then the floors, walls, and roof. The most fundamental axiom from which our thinking can grow is this: "The World Exists."

This may seem obvious, but beginning an inquiry with superficial assumptions is far riskier than starting at profound depth. While this axiom may appear to conflict with the understanding of the universe as empty or unified, true communion with that emptiness paradoxically deepens our relationship with existence itself. It becomes a more radical and vibrant kind of existence.

To build the strongest foundation, we must begin by excavating—digging deeply into the mental ground we stand on. Only after clearing the debris of prior assumptions can we pour the concrete of enduring principles. So, for now, clear your mind. Set aside everything you think you know about grazing, ranching, or anything else. It will still be there when you're done reading.

FOUNDATIONS FOR ECOLOGICAL THOUGHT

What follows is a series of nine principles, each building upon the last, starting with the most fundamental. I'll present each proposition, explore its meaning, and then illustrate how it relates to our work in interacting with landscapes. While some may not immediately appear relevant to the task at hand, their purpose is to establish a mental framework grounded in reality—one strong enough to guide sustainable action.

As we approach practical landscape management, I will offer questions that demonstrate how these principles can serve as filters for decision-making.

1. ***The world exists:***

   This is the most basic axiom of our philosophical framework. It may sound obvious, but its implications run deeper than we often realize. Many people, whether consciously or unconsciously, behave as though the world doesn't truly exist. Phrases like "Your truth is just as valid as mine" reflect a relativist mindset that subtly denies the world's objective reality.

Relativism challenges us to ask, "Is there another way to see this?" It can help break down rigid thought structures, but if taken too far, it becomes a trap. You get stuck in endless questioning, unable to commit to anything—classic nihilism. In Western philosophy, that's where it often leads. In Zen, they call it "Enlightenment Sickness."

Let me give you an example that's stuck with me.

During undergrad at the University of Oregon, I took a Philosophy of Human Nature class. On the first day, the professor walked in and stood silently at the front of a packed auditorium—300 wide-eyed students, completely unaware of what was about to hit them.

Once we settled down, he spoke. "Raise your hand if you think it's okay to believe whatever you want."

Most of the room raised their hand. These students were West Coast kids who'd been raised on "live and let live."

I didn't raise mine. Not because I was particularly smart—just because I knew how to smell a trick question.

The professor didn't say a word. He calmly walked over to the computer, hit a button, and—

Boom. A giant Nazi flag filled the screen.

"Now," he said, "how many of you still think it's okay to believe whatever you want?"

2. **The world is discoverable:**

   If we're going to say or know anything about the world, we have to assume it's something we can grasp—that we're built to interact with and make sense of it. This implies that the structure of the world and the structure of our minds share a basic compatibility. If that weren't true, nothing we observed would mean anything.

   The fact that we can study and understand the world gives us the same opportunity with grazing animals and ecosystems. Through this, we gain the tools to participate more consciously in the processes of life.

3. **The world is governed by consistent physical laws:**

   If the universe is truly discoverable, it has to behave in ways that can be recognized and understood. Patterns and phenomena emerge that we can define, categorize, and share with others. This consistency is the foundation of science, allowing us to build knowledge and develop practices that work over time.

4. **The natural world is shaped by billions of years of continuous evolution and dynamic forces:**

   Think of the universe as a vast, ongoing experiment. Trillions of interactions—chemical, physical, magnetic, and more—have played out over eons, resulting in the complex and interconnected reality we inhabit today. What exists now is the cumulative outcome of this cosmic experimentation.

5. **In the natural world, grazing animals and their predators function as eco-mechanisms:**

   Grazing animals serve vital ecological functions such as grazing, nutrient cycling, and soil fertilization. These processes form the foundation of our work as land managers. For these functions to operate properly, grazing animals must be paired with adequate predation. This balance leads us to explore the deeper relationship between humanity and two of the core forces driving ecological health.

   Reflect on this: "Am I considering grazing animals as integral ecological forces or simply as a protein source for human consumption?"

6. **Human civilization is a derivative of the natural world:**

   This principle reinforces the idea that human civilization and the natural world are inseparable. Our understanding of cattle and their role should be rooted in their ecological importance, not merely as a resource for human consumption. Consuming organisms is just one aspect of ecological function.

   We all have two roles on this planet: Our active role (contributing to our ecological niche) and our passive role (returning to the system as nutrients upon death). Since all organisms eventually return to the Earth, it makes more sense to base ecosystem management decisions on the role of organisms in the ecosystem rather than viewing them solely as commodities.

Failing to view cattle as part of the flesh of ecology arises from the perspective that human civilization is separate from the natural world. When we view ourselves as distinct from nature, we limit our understanding and miss the deeper ecological connections.

Reflect on this: "Am I considering human civilization as an inseparable part of the natural world, or as something separate from it?"

7. **The natural world, and therefore human civilization, is disproportionately influenced by key ecological mechanisms:**

   Not all ecological mechanisms have the same level of influence within a system. While any change in the system will affect it, the impact of that change is not equally distributed. A vole plays an important role, but the effect of a thundering herd of bison crossing the landscape is much more significant.

   Recognizing that the activities of grazing animals (the herd effect) have a disproportionately large influence on ecosystem function is critical to managing landscapes in ways that preserve and enhance ecological health. This positive impact extends beyond the environment and influences human civilization as well.

   Reflect on this: "Am I focusing my attention and efforts on the most significant ecological mechanisms, the ones that have the greatest potential to move the system in the right direction?"

8. **"Cattle function as a protein source" is a derivative proposition:**

   When constructing a functional philosophy, it's essential to determine whether an idea is foundational or derivative. If an idea is derivative, it must not be allowed to occupy the same space as the foundational principles of a paradigm.

   Reflect on this: "Am I allowing my concern for the beef product to hinder the ecological potential of my landscape?"

9. **Considering cattle as a protein source creates distorted outcomes:**

   This principle highlights the negative consequences of reducing cattle to mere commodities. This approach results in harmful externalities such as deforestation, habitat destruction, and climate destabilization. When protein is prioritized, or even treated equally with ecological processes, it leads to negative ecological outcomes. A balanced worldview, however, produces more predictable and mutually reinforcing outcomes for all system components. In other words, prioritizing ecology first leads to more sustainable, beneficial beef production outcomes.

   Reflect on this: "Grazing can be used to stimulate almost any ecosystem, but are the effects of grazing creating negative ecological outcomes? If so, am I violating any of the more fundamental principles stated here?"

These key components are essential for developing and understanding a system that functions as a whole. They are consistent, coherent, and non-contradictory. Decision-making in grazing management, and by extension food production, should be evaluated through these principles to identify contradictions, incompatibilities, and inconsistencies. At first, you may need to revisit these principles to refine your thinking, but over time, their application will become second nature.

It's important to note that these principles are not gospel; they are simply a reflection of how I view the world. They result from my efforts to create a fully coherent mental model for achieving positive ecological and economic outcomes. Any model that aligns more closely with reality should, by definition, produce the desired outcomes when followed properly.

CATTLE AS DRIVERS OF ECOSYSTEMS

> *"Where there is no vision, the people perish:*
> *but he that keepeth the law, happy is he."*
>
> ***- Proverbs 29:18***

The Perils of Misguided Thinking

A common refrain in the grazing community is that cattle serve two purposes:

1. Transform grass into protein; and
2. Drive, maintain, and harmonize ecosystem function.

On the surface, these two ideas may seem equally valid. Cattle are both protein sources and drivers of ecosystem health. However, when considered together, this dual purpose creates a philosophical tension: One cannot serve two masters.

There are hidden dangers in constructing a system based on the assumption that both claims—cattle as protein sources and cattle as ecosystem drivers—are equally valid. If they aren't, the paradigm can lead to distortions that create inefficiencies and unintended consequences, ultimately impacting the long-term sustainability of the system.

Consider the example of Concentrated Animal Feeding Operations (CAFOs), or feedlots. These systems aim to streamline protein production by bringing in feed grown through monoculture, which on the surface seems efficient. However, it's akin to tunneling through a mountain, cutting down a forest, and damming a river to build a nature park—this approach is a shortcut that overlooks the broader, interconnected ecological processes. It may work in the short term, but it misses the more complex, sustainable interactions that can lead to lasting ecological health.

Here's a simplified version of the resource pathway in the modern industrial beef system: Natural gas is converted (using fossil energy) into nitrogen fertilizer, which is then transported to monoculture tillage fields. These fields typically focus on a single crop grown for animal feed. After applying herbicides, the crops are harvested and sent to feedlots, where cattle are confined for the final fattening portion of their life. Cattle typically spend their first year or more on pasture before being moved to feedlots. In the feedlot, they are confined and fed the feed brought in from these monoculture systems. Once the cattle reach their desired weight or their allotted days on a finishing ration, they are slaughtered, processed, and delivered to local grocers, providing protein for the consumer.

This system is designed for efficiency, focusing on maximizing production to meet human demand. However, it simplifies the complex, interconnected processes of nature, which can lead to long-term ecological consequences.

This system may work for a time, but the unnatural pressures placed on the landscape will eventually lead to its decline. The carbon and nutrient stocks, instead of being cycled, shared, and redistributed, are extracted and diverted into a human-managed system. Once these resources enter the human system, they are unlikely to be reintegrated effectively into the broader ecology.

In essence, once we extract the carbon, nutrients, and minerals from the landscape, it's unlikely the landscape will receive them again for a long time.

In this scenario, we treat the land as an endless resource, extracting from it without giving back. To keep it productive, we rely on fertilizers and herbicides, especially as the landscape begins to show signs of stress. After decades (or even centuries) of heavy reliance on these inputs, the system becomes dependent on them. Forcing a system to yield at the expense of its long-term health is not only unsustainable, but ultimately ineffective. The system will eventually break down. What happens when these inputs no longer provide the same results?

A wiser approach would be to move away from this purely extractive relationship and return a significant portion of the proceeds to the land. Giving our fields and pastures as much of the resources they provide as possible is a more sustainable strategy. Taking only what we need is always good advice.

The system described above is the natural outcome of viewing cattle primarily as a protein source. While all living beings serve as food for others in the food chain, this concept takes a back seat when we consider our role in managing large landscapes. Large herbivores, in relation to human civilization, are not just a source of protein—they are dynamic, living mechanisms for ecological maintenance.

To truly activate this system, we need to embrace the role of predators—not just as passive consumers, but as active participants in the ecosystem. Being a predator means engaging with the land in a way that is in tune with its rhythms, driving the processes that sustain and renew the landscape.

The Guiding Truth

I propose this fundamental thesis as the foundation of my thoughts on the subject:

> ***Cattle are ecological maintainers, and humans must act as their partners, protectors, and predators.***

This doesn't mean we cannot eat beef. In fact, it's quite the opposite. If we approach this correctly, we will have more beef than we could ever need. The problem arises when beef production becomes the primary driver of our systems. Starting with that imperative is like trying to gather rainwater at the top of a mountain. It is much wiser to simply position ourselves where it naturally flows.

I want to make it very clear: ***If we manage cattle without making the beef product the primary focus, we will end up with more beef than we currently produce.***

The dual perspectives that cattle are both protein sources AND ecological drivers represent two different ways of viewing cattle's relationship with the fabric of reality. One perspective aligns more closely with a properly constructed mental model: the ecological role of cattle as maintainers of ecosystems. The protein aspect naturally follows from this ecological function. How do we know which perspective is more aligned with a functional model? We can ask ourselves which perspective, when used as a foundation, can support additional ideas without creating contradictions. In other words: which building block can support the most ideas without causing the entire structure to collapse?

I emphasize this point because changing old ways of thinking can be difficult. You cannot operate from a new understanding bolted onto an old one. To truly make progress, we must dig deep, discard outdated ideas, and rebuild from the ground up.

We all have pre-existing neural pathways for the concepts we regularly use. These pathways are often shaped without much reflection on what we know or how we know it, and usually, they remain unconscious.

To generate new understanding, we need to find a

way to step around these established pathways. While the brain will naturally change with exposure to new ideas, real change comes when we actively challenge our current frameworks. By examining an idea at its conceptual core, we're more likely to develop propositions that lead to a more accurate mental model of reality.

This is why Tom Lasater, the legendary rancher who developed the Beefmaster breed, said, "I would rather make a rancher out of a boy off the streets of New York or Tokyo than a boy raised on a conventional ranch."

In the same vein, Henry David Thoreau famously said, "Farms are far more easily gotten than gotten rid of."

Humanity has long, though perhaps implicitly, based its relationship with cattle on the idea that "cow = protein." While this has given rise to rich and fascinating cultures—such as the vaquero or cowboy of the American West and the Gauchos of South America—it has also, at best, failed to reverse the decline of our grazing lands. At worst, it has contributed to that decline.

It is said that cowboys in West Texas used to change horses at midday as the horses grew tired from pushing through the tall grass. This is no longer the case. Many ranchers claim to be the original environmentalists, asserting that their well-being depends on the land and that landscape health is their top priority. Yet, this idea is hard to reconcile with the reality that our landscapes are much less healthy today than they were a century ago.

Modern ranching culture is currently trying to address environmental decline by adding a surface-level focus on "sustainability" or "responsibility" to the deeply ingrained, protein-centered ethos. However, this linear evolution is ineffective. It's akin to the incremental changes made to the engines of the Boeing 737 airframe, which eventually led to the 737 MAX disasters—where the attempts at improvement were ultimately overshadowed by the underlying flaws in the design.

Boeing introduced the 737 in 1967 and then produced over 10,000 of these aircraft over the next 50 years, making it the most profitable aircraft line in the company's history—essentially a cash cow.

The first challenge to this cash cow came in 2014 when Airbus released the A320neo, a more fuel-efficient short-haul aircraft. In an effort to maintain market share, Boeing quickly responded with the 737 MAX, which promised a 15% improvement in fuel efficiency. However, in their rush to compete with Airbus, both Boeing and the Federal Aviation Administration encountered significant issues related to cost-cutting, regulatory oversight, and a lack of transparency.[4]

In October 2018, Lion Air Flight 610 took off from Jakarta, Indonesia, only to crash into the Java Sea, tragically killing all 189 passengers and crew. Five months later, Ethiopian Airlines Flight 302 took off from Addis Ababa, Ethiopia. The plane crashed shortly after takeoff, resulting in the deaths of all 157 people on board.

---

4. Bhattacharya, Subhendu, and Y. Nisha. "A Case Study on Boeing's 737 MAX Crisis on Account of Leadership Failure." International Journal of Research in Engineering, Science and Management 3.9 (2020): 116-118.

Both aircraft were Boeing 737 MAX planes, equipped with the MCAS system—a software program designed to correct the inherent instability of the airframe caused by the increased size and repositioning of the engines. In both cases, the pilots were unfamiliar with the system, and when it activated unnecessarily, they did not know how to deactivate it. Production of the 737 MAX was halted in December 2019, pending further investigation.[5]

Boeing's stock price dropped by 23%, and its market capitalization fell by $55 billion. Dennis Muilenburg was ousted as CEO amid charges of "gross mismanagement." This marked the beginning of a prolonged period of difficulty for the Boeing brand, the effects of which are still being felt today.

At its core, Boeing made the critical mistake of prioritizing short-term solutions over long-term redesign. Instead of taking the necessary and inevitable step of completely reworking the airframe, they opted for a series of small, incremental adjustments that ultimately left the aircraft dangerously unstable.

The protein-centric commodification of cattle remains dominant, and the language of "sustainability" risks becoming little more than a superficial fix—a "new engine on the same old airframe," much like Boeing's attempts to continually upgrade the 737. Just as those planes eventually experienced catastrophic failures, our ranching systems are on track for inevitable breakdowns if we focus on

---

5. Johnston, Phillip, and Rozi Harris. "The Boeing 737 MAX saga: lessons for software organizations." Software Quality Professional 21.3 (2019): 4-12.

performance without addressing the underlying flaws in the system. This creates a contradiction in ranching and farming culture, where the language of progress obscures deeper systemic issues.

While the commodity market has undeniably served a valuable purpose and will continue to play an important role in the future, we must carefully evaluate the principles that underpin these markets. This reflection is necessary to ensure they evolve in alignment with more sustainable and holistic approaches to land management.

We have pushed the existing system to its limits, and we cannot continue increasing efficiency or output without a fundamental redesign that aligns with nature's operating system. Our current system and efforts at improvement are misaligned with how nature truly operates, and anything that is poorly aligned will inevitably collapse under the weight of reality.

In the grazing industry, I often hear practitioners talk about a need for "balance" or "connection" between grazing and ecology. But more often than not, this is used as a way to delay addressing the deeper issues and keep the status quo intact. The idea of grazing and ecology coexisting is a misleading contradiction.

To suggest they are separate by claiming they must "connect" is to reinforce the division between them. In reality, grazing activity and ecological processes are so intertwined that it's inappropriate to view them as separate entities. Even using the word "connection" can mislead us, setting us down a path of mental fragmentation. We don't think of grazing elk and the ecosystem as "coexisting"; the grazing elk *are* the ecology. While human consciousness often creates separation, it also has the potential to transcend and integrate it. This is one of the profound aspects of truly understanding the systems at play.

Slogans like "sustainable ranching" and "responsible ranching" often reveal an underlying philosophy: that ranching is beneficial to us, but potentially harmful to nature unless we get it just right. The implied message is that humanity receives from nature, but only if nature is carefully managed and treated "correctly." Nature, in this framework, is seen as the giver, and humanity as the receiver. This perspective assumes a separation between the two—nature is something to be controlled or managed, while we are the ones benefiting.

What we need, however, is a system where both humanity and nature are both beneficiaries and benefactors. This requires us to dissolve the conceptual separation between man and nature, and between agriculture and ecology. Instead of simply receiving benefits from nature, we need to recognize that we are active participants in a system where our actions help nurture and sustain the ecology. The true challenge lies not in managing nature to benefit us, but in creating a relationship where both humanity and nature thrive together. Only then can we build a system where feedback loops are so aligned that nature benefits even when human actions are imperfect.

The majority of our environmental and conservation efforts are built on the lifeless gravel of conceptual separation, rather than the fertile ground of unity. Terms like "wilderness," "preserves," and "conservation areas" imply a divide between us and the land, pushing us to see nature as something separate, distant, and to be managed apart from human life. In doing so, we condemn both the land and ourselves to a stagnant, disconnected existence.

This approach does not nourish the life of nature; instead, it restricts its vitality, much like a premature mummification. It cuts off the flow of energy and creativity that could breathe life back into the land. As the saying goes, "Anything not busy being born is busy dying." Without renewal, new relationships, and fresh energy, the systems we call "nature" will gradually lose their vitality.

If a race car driver sees themselves as separate from the car, they will at best never win a race, and at worst, crash and die. As a species, we must learn to operate in our natural home from a place of unity, understanding that we are an integral part of the system, not apart from it. In the conventional "sustainability" narrative, we often observe, interpret, and act under the assumption that grazing and the environment are separate. This mindset is ingrained and predictable. How can we move beyond this and embrace a more integrated, holistic approach?

Pastoralism urgently needs a unifying theme that transcends traditional divides: a paradigm shift that resolves the tension between grazing and ecology, making the separation between them conceptually irrelevant. This shift must be both an aspirational and invitational vision—built on the belief in a reality that is infinitely repeatable and sustainable.

We must work to dissolve the boundary between grazing and ecology, both in our minds and in practice. To do this, we need a clearer guiding light—a more precisely defined north star—through which we can channel our decision-making and align ourselves with the vast, interconnected reality of the natural world.

In this new narrative, we must allow the separation to dissolve by revitalizing a forgotten mythological narrative that humanity was born from the herds.

And from this foundation, I offer the following as a way forward that transcends the separation between grazing and ecology:

Herds exist to maintain and enhance ecosystem processes.

At the start of my grazing journey, I made a deliberate decision to relegate the "beef quality outcome" to little more than an afterthought. I asked myself, "What if I viewed beef not even as a byproduct of a healthy, functioning ecosystem, but as a waste product?" This shift in perspective helped me uncover the hidden assumptions and incentives that come from a desire to meet contemporary market demands and customer preferences. But here's the amazing part... When management decisions are made with the aim of harmonizing with nature, they naturally lead to better quality beef—higher fat content and more nutrient-dense protein. We'll explore this more in depth later.

It's in the long-term interest of both the producer and humanity-at-large to focus on cattle and beef produced with the right mindset—herds of cattle existing to maintain and enhance ecosystem processes. We must resist the temptation to let the "quality" of beef (a subjective standard often influenced by ego and fashion) shape our management decisions.

"But the market doesn't want the type of cattle you're talking about," you might say.

You may be right, but I can think of no better reply than the words of Ralph Waldo Emerson: "God will not have his work made manifest by cowards."

The modern industrial market rewards systems that degrade ecosystems, with its profitability supported by the diminishing natural assets of land stewards. While it is not the result of nefarious intentions, it is still a problematic reality. It is up to us to cultivate a new market—one that rewards ecosystem improvement rather than exploitation. Yes, auction houses typically undervalue cattle bred for eco-maintenance. That's because they are designed to support an industrial system that rewards cattle fitting a particular mold. Shorter, heavier cattle may not fit that mold, but they are exactly what our landscapes need. The good news is that managing cattle operations in harmony with the land will ultimately lead to more profit, even with these discounted cattle, because our costs are lower and our stocking rates are higher.

We must also recognize that external forces aren't the only drivers of market change. While they can certainly support transformation, real and lasting change can also arise from internal forces. The cathode ray television wasn't replaced because of government regulation—it was replaced because someone invented a better television, and the market embraced it. Similarly, Tesla Motors isn't trying to revolutionize the automobile industry by simply making an electric car; they are focused on making a better car. As landscape managers (formerly known as beef producers) increasingly realize the undeniable truth that aligning with ecological processes leads to more profitable outcomes, the market will evolve. Does this vision sound impossible?

It's not. It's the natural consequence of orienting human-managed grazing toward ecological realities.

Now that we've established the foundational principles guiding our perspective, it's time to explore the deep historical and mythological connections between herds, humanity, and ecology.

With these principles in place, we turn to one of the most enduring and transformative relationships in ecological history: the bond between herds and humanity. This connection is not just a reflection of ecological unity; it is the key to understanding how grazing has shaped our landscapes and played a pivotal role in humanity's evolution. It is such a powerful force that we may be entirely justified in saying it is the heartbeat of ecology and the foundation of humanity's place in a green and thriving world.

II. HUMANS
PARTNER, PROTECTOR, PREDATOR

LEGENDS OF THE HERD

"... when the rime melted into drops, there was made thereof a cow, which hight Audhumbla. Four milk–streams ran from her teats, and she fed Ymer.

Thereupon asked Ganglere: On what did the cow subsist?

Answered Har: She licked the salt–stones that were covered with rime, and the first day that she licked the stones there came out of them in the evening a man's hair, the second day a man's head, and the third day the whole man was there. This man's name was Bure; he was fair of face, great and mighty..."

- Prose Edda

Ymir Suckling the Cow Audhumla, c. 1775–78; Nicolai Abraham Abildgaard (Danish, 1743–1809); oil on canvas, Statens Museum for Kunst, Copenhagen; public domain.

The Prose Edda, a foundational text in Norse Mythology, tells the story of Audhumbla, the primordial cow. In the beginning, only fire and ice exist. When these elements meet, they produce "elemental drops." From the first drop, Ymer emerges, embodying raw, chaotic potential. He is also the father of the Jotnar, supernatural beings who often oppose the Gods. The second drop forms Audhumbla, the great cow, from whose teats flow four streams of milk to nourish the hungry Ymer. Eventually, Ymer is slain, and his body becomes the Earth itself—he is the landscape.

Ymer embodies both the potential for and the substance of the landscape. This suggests the unity of potential and substance—they are one and the same. This resonates with the universal experiences of awakening, where many have sensed that the vast universe is both empty and teeming with dynamic energy.

Ymer, embodying both potential and its realization, cannot sustain himself. Audhumbla, however, is the nurturer, the provider of energy. She facilitates growth, maintenance, and transformation. She is the life-giving force—the Great Maintainer. Landscapes, like all systems, cannot sustain themselves without a framework—an operating system. Audhumbla, then, represents this system, providing the structure for the continual cycle of potential turning into substance, life into death, and something into nothing, only to begin again.

Let us apply this idea to one of the most crucial mechanisms for ecological maintenance—herds of animals migrating across a savanna. We've all seen footage of herds sweeping across African landscapes. It's no mystery that herds graze the grass, and after they pass, little grass remains. While it may be hard to grasp at first, this simple concept is foundational to human history and echoes throughout our shared human experience.

The herd acts as the destructive force in the short term, the creative force in the medium term, and the sustaining force in the long term. The herd sweeps through, consuming the grass and resetting the landscape, creating the conditions for a burgeoning order to emerge. This process activates latent energy in the system, sparking a rebirth. Over time, the new order becomes stagnant, and chaos begins to creep in. Danger and unpredictability fill the deepening chaotic niche. This could be predators in the tall grass, the threat of fire, or an infestation. As systems atrophy, they inevitably attract decomposing forces—some of which are far less beneficial than a herd of herbivores. Then, ideally, the herd returns, consuming the grass which pushes back the chaos and brings fresh life and a new order. This cycle repeats, continually renewing the landscape.

Returning to the story: In the Prose Edda, the disguised King Ganglere asks how the cow sustains herself, and it is revealed that Audhumbla survives by licking rime-covered salt stones. Over the course of three days, her licking uncovers a man. On the first day, she uncovers hair; on the second, a head; and on the third, a full body. The man she uncovers is Buri, who becomes the forefather of the Gods. Thor, foremost among them, is destined to be the creator of humankind.

So, in this seemingly simple story, we see the creation of the necessary preconditions for life itself to emerge and begin the process of awakening human consciousness. From a more literal interpretation, the instinctive and natural actions of a herd animal—symbolized by the cow—created the conditions for the emergence of humanity, the being who possesses consciousness and the potential for awakening.

History is full of examples where migratory herbivores play a key role in indigenous mythology. Two additional examples highlight this.

The first is the creation myth of the Tungus people, a Siberian indigenous culture. They believe that the Earth was once covered by water. Gradually, rocks began to emerge from the water, bearing a striking resemblance to the rime-covered rocks in the Audhumbla story. When these rocks appeared, primeval Elk and Reindeer (likely Mammoths) emerged from the water. The tracks of the "wild reindeer" were said to have transformed into rivers, and their footsteps became lakes. The 'water' in the beginning of this story can be interpreted as the primordial void—the unknowable, precosmogonic past. Once again, we find a culture positioning the herd animal as the very force responsible for creating a livable world—the ecology.

This myth complements another Siberian creation story beautifully. This version goes as follows: In the beginning, people did not live on Earth; they resided in Heaven. The birth of Earth-bound humanity began when a young woman defied her fate. Refusing an arranged marriage to an old man because she was in love with a younger one, she was cast out of Heaven. Her father possessed a very old reindeer, which he gave her for the journey. She descended to Earth on its back, marking the beginning of human life on the planet.

The reindeer, very old, soon grew tired. He could no longer keep his footing and began tumbling uncontrollably toward Earth. The maiden became frightened, and the reindeer spoke to her in a human voice. He instructed the girl to pull out all his hair and scatter it on the ocean as they tumbled downward. Each strand turned into a log, and the reindeer landed on the largest one. He then instructed the woman to gather all the logs and arrange them into a raft. Though they now had a rudimentary foundation, the vast expanse of water surrounded them. To feed herself and the reindeer, she fashioned loops and nets from the reindeer's hair to catch fish.

This continued for some time. Then, one day, the reindeer told the young woman that he had grown too old and would soon die. He instructed her to kill him proactively, saying that if she did not, she would die as well. He further told her to lay his skin on the water so it could become land. He directed her to scatter his hair, which would turn into a forest. The reindeer then told her to preserve his lice so they could become new reindeer to populate this land. "Without reindeer, you will not live a single day," he said.

So, the young woman followed his instructions and killed the old reindeer. Everything he foretold came true, and his dying breath became the wind. In a final act of creation, the reindeer's two lungs transformed into the first Earth-bound man and woman.[6]

While this story may initially seem as nonsensical as Audhumbla the Primordial Cow, it offers a profound depiction of the harmony between humanity and herd animals. Though the young woman in the story is described as human, she is far more—a type of goddess. Her refusal to marry an old man and instead fall in love with a younger one symbolizes the divine drive toward renewal and revivification. The emergence of a metaphysical herd animal on the surface of the Earth, accompanied by a cast-out goddess, speaks to the anointed role of herd animals to

---

6. V.A.Robbeck, Descriptions of reindeer in Even myths. Folklore and Ethnography of indigenous peoples of the North, Leningrad, 1986.

perform a grand mission—bringing order and form to the primordial void.

The inseparable bond between herd animals and humanity is highlighted when the reindeer speaks to the girl in a human voice. This communication allows for perfect understanding. Understanding and harmony are intrinsically linked. The first sign of a herd animal transforming the inhospitable void into a habitable world comes when he instructs her to scatter his hair, which then becomes logs.

The second instance of revivification triumphing over atrophy occurs when the reindeer instructs the young woman to sacrifice him in order to create habitable land and the first people. The body of the herd animal—its flesh and blood, as well as its activity—brings the habitable world into existence. The dance reaches its climax when the reindeer urges the young woman to understand that without the reindeer—their bodies and their actions—no one will survive a single day.

It is only with these preconditions laid out that the first man and woman can occupy the physical and spiritual world that has been constructed for them. It's a beautiful and poetic sentiment that as the reindeer let out his dying breath, that breath became the wind.

This story reflects a deeper truth: humanity must not only passively preserve nature, but actively participate in the cycles of life and death. Just as the young woman had to proactively kill the reindeer to give life to the Earth, we too must willingly engage with the natural systems around us. While it's obviously beneficial to protect nature, we must not simply wall it off. Doing so runs the risk of allowing systems to atrophy if we fail to actively participate in the ongoing rejuvenation they require.

There is an element of orderly predestination in the unfolding of these stories. It reflects the old trope of the Universe coming to know itself. Humanity was birthed from the Earth, with herd animals as the midwives. Life operates on a gradual spectrum of consciousness and awareness, but there was a clear qualitative shift when humanity emerged in the savannas of old. Life that is conscious of its own existence, with the capacity to make decisions and consciously reshape its environment, belongs to a different order than life that operates purely through instinct.

We find ourselves in a unique position, having been gifted the profound gift of consciousness and the potential for deeper levels of awakening. This awareness places upon us the responsibility of maintaining and enhancing the world that gave rise to our existence.

BACK TO THE SAVANNA: A PLEISTOCENE BLUEPRINT

The human brain and our collective experience were shaped and continue to be influenced by our relationship with herds. To truly understand this, we need to revisit the Pleistocene Savanna. Contrary to popular belief, the Pleistocene—often thought of simply as "The Ice Age"—wasn't just a barren wasteland. From 2.6 million years ago to 12,800 years ago, the planet experienced four cycles of glacial expansion and contraction. Through all of this, one constant remained:

the presence of herds of megaherbivores, their predators, and the dynamic savanna ecosystem that their interactions helped shape.

We must also define the term 'savanna.' A savanna is a type of wooded grassland. It can range from sparse savannas with scattered trees to denser ones where trees are more tightly spaced. Regardless of density, the defining characteristic of a savanna is that the trees are spaced far enough apart to allow sunlight to reach the ground, nurturing a grassy understory beneath.

Megaherbivores: Architects of Renewal

Nature doesn't evolve toward Savanna without a dedicated team of landscapers. We all know what happens when we neglect mowing the yard. Herd animals, moving in tight groups, are the ones that have historically (and, in rare cases, still do) maintain and nourish these park-like ecosystems. Their movement prevents trees from becoming too dense and blocking sunlight from reaching the ground, while also maintaining the grasslands under the trees. Additionally, their digestive systems keep the understory healthy and cycling. Without herds of megaherbivores, moist environments typically shift toward overgrown forests filled with woody shrubs, briars, and vines—much like what we see in the current American Southeast or Southeast Asia. Similarly, in drier, more seasonal environments, the absence of megaherbivores leads to the transformation of savannas into simple grasslands and eventually deserts.[7]

7. Ruyle, G. B. (2000). Holistic Management: A New Framework for Decision

The mastodon plays a key role in this story. Archaeological evidence suggests that the mastodon primarily fed on browse—shrubs, leaves, and coniferous twigs.[8] Anyone who has observed herbivores knows they tend to prefer fresh, young forage and will often graze it before other types of available forage. This behavior extends to browse as well. It is likely that one of the mastodon's favorite food sources was saplings. Herds of mastodon, in this way, acted as roving bands of tree pruners, removing saplings and pruning mature trees. Browsing animals also apply significant pressure on woody shrubs, which serve both as food and as convenient scratching posts for the tall megaherbivores. I've seen cows finish scratching a young tree or shrub only for the next in the herd to continue. By the time the herd has moved on, the tree has been reduced to a mere nub.

These activities exerted significant pressure on trees and woody shrubs. By maintaining this pressure, mastodons and other megaherbivores facilitated large, open-canopy landscapes, allowing sunlight to reach plants at the soil's surface, though not necessarily continuously. This dynamic helped keep the carbon cycle active and ensured the ecosystem remained populated and functional. Elephants today continue to play a similar role on the African Savanna, though in much smaller numbers than were historically present.

Making, Second Edition, Edited by Allan Savory, with Jody Butterfield, Island Press, Washington, DC, 1999.

8. NEW YORK STATE MUSEUM: The Cohoes Mastodon. (n.d.). http://exhibitions.nysm.nysed.gov/cohesmastodon/phone/mastodon-facts.html

FERMENTATION VS OXIDATION: THE BATTLE FOR RENEWAL

To truly understand the vital role these megaherbivores played in maintaining healthy savanna habitats, we must first grasp how forage cycles. Forage, including grass and forbs, can cycle in two primary ways: through fermentation (biological decay) or oxidation (chemical decay).

Fermentation

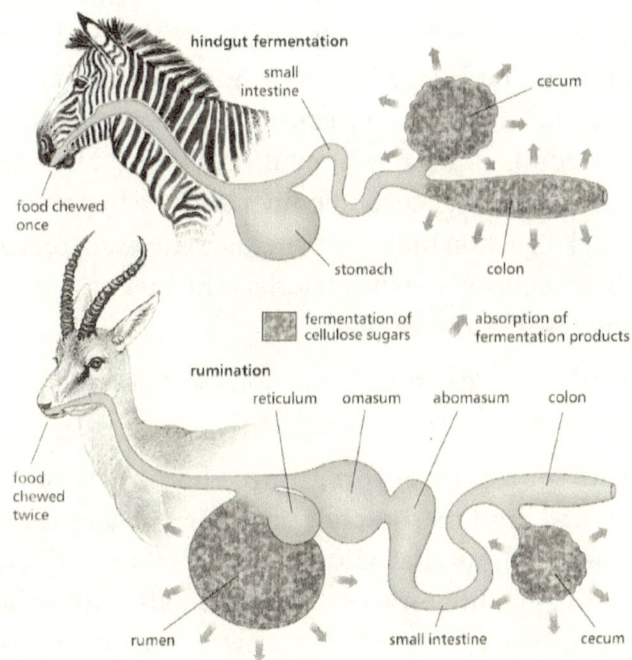

Stylized comparison of hindgut fermentation and rumination digestive systems, by Bryan Shorrocks (2007); from The Biology of African Savannahs (Oxford

Univ. Press), reprinted in Brian J. Huntley, Herbivory: Mammalian Grazers and Browsers (2023); licensed under CC BY 4.0. Available at: https://www.researchgate.net/figure/Stylised-comparison-of-hindgut-fermentation-and-rumination-digestive-systems-From_fig2_369076091

Herbivorous fermentation occurs through two main digestive technologies: foregut fermentation and hindgut fermentation. The most advanced form of foregut fermentation is rumination. Cattle, bison, sheep, goats, deer, wildebeest, antelope, and giraffes are all examples of ruminants. However, more primitive forms of foregut fermentation are found in animals like the kangaroo.

Ruminants have four sections in their digestive system, with the first being the rumen. Think of it like an on-board fermentation tank. The rumen is home to microbes that digest the forage the animal consumes. These microbes are essential for breaking down cellulose, the sugar that forms plant cell walls. The dead microbes and the byproducts of microbial digestion then pass into the reticulum, omasum, and abomasum, where the material is further broken down and absorbed by the animal.

In other words: ruminants don't eat grass. They use grass to feed their food!

Hind-gut fermenters, like elephants, horses, mammoths, and mastodons (both current and extinct), have large colons that allow them to extract nutrients from lower-quality forages. These animals are the heavy lifters in forage cycling. Many are aware that giving horses unrestricted access to fresh pasture, which can be OK for cattle, can lead to colic or even death—they're built for tougher, rougher forage.

The two fermentation systems—foregut and hindgut fermentation—worked together to clear the forage each season, allowing for fresh regrowth during the growing season. Ruminants consumed the more palatable, high-protein forage, while hindgut fermenters took the less-palatable, lower-protein, stemmy plants. Of course, all animals will graze preferentially, but from a landscape perspective, these bio-digestive systems created a perfect partnership for effective forage cycling.

It should be noted that modern grazing lands are characterized by a massive shortage of hind-gut fermenters. This is one of the primary reasons for landscape degradation. We simply don't have the animals needed to take down the less desirable parts of plants. In a sense, a properly oriented grazing system will seek to satisfy the ecological requirements historically delivered by hindgut fermenters.

This can be done by adding protein supplements to a group of ruminants, which allows them to cycle the higher-fiber plants while also selecting and breeding cattle that demonstrate a genetic propensity to stay in suitable body condition on high-fiber forages. In other words, we need to help the ruminants mimic the role of hindgut fermenters and breed cattle that thrive on rougher forage.

Oxidation

Oxidation can occur in two primary ways: quickly or slowly. Imagine a stand of yellow, dead grass, its slender stems swaying gently in the breeze. This is an example of slow oxidation. It typically happens over time when plants die, go dormant, or become stressed by drought. Oxidation occurs when the production of free radicals exceeds the plant's ability to neutralize them. These free radicals—molecules with unpaired electrons—accumulate and damage cell membranes and pigments, ultimately leading to cell death. In essence, plants become overwhelmed by free radicals, which cause oxidative stress by stealing electrons from healthy cells.

Fast oxidation, on the other hand, is fire—a destructive force that accelerates the process.

All life forms rely on the energy stored in the bonds between carbon atoms and other atoms, which is released when organic molecules are metabolized. When living material is digested biologically, the energy stored in carbon-based molecules is immediately available as fuel for various forms of life. If a plant oxidizes and its carbon escapes to the atmosphere, that energy is lost to the system and must re-enter the food web through another plant, creating inefficiency and systemic entropy. In other words, the more planetary carbon dioxide is converted biologically, the more energy becomes available to sustain biological processes.

Fire

The idea that controlled burns are a critical part of the natural ecology is ubiquitous because we have cultural amnesia to the role that megaherbivores played in keeping our wooded parkland ecology open and maintained. It was only after the Younger Dryas (12,800 YBP to 11,400 YBP), when the vast majority of megaherbivores went extinct, that we began the regular application of controlled burns to keep landscapes open and woody shrubs in check.

There is an exception to this, however, which can be found in Australia's ecological history. There is evidence and an oral history of controlled burns being used as far as 40,000 years ago. It is also worth noting that the megaherbivores of Australia experienced an extinction event around that time—almost certainly from human overkill. The overkill hypothesis seems perfectly acceptable in Australia's case but is lacking as an adequate explanation for the planet-wide Holocene Extinction Event which occurred around the Younger Dryas Boundary (12,800 years ago).

As the science currently stands, I find myself most amply moved by the Younger Dryas Impact Hypothesis, which posits that a disintegrating comet intercepted our northern hemisphere at that time. This impact resulted in widespread death and destruction, and a 1400-year spell of temperatures 10°C lower than usual. In essence, Miami became Boston overnight. For more on this topic, the *Comet Research Group* has a wealth of information.

From a thermodynamic and ecological efficiency standpoint, I view the frequent use of deliberate revivifying fire as a suboptimal strategy for landscape management, despite its broad acceptance within academic and land management circles. This use of fire appears desirable only in the absence of large herds of herbivores that perform a similar, but more effective, ecological function. These massive forage cycling herds began declining near the end of the Pleistocene then suddenly went extinct around

12,800 years ago at the onset of the Younger Dryas Period. In this period, an estimated 82% of megafauna (any animal with a mass of greater than 40kg) went extinct in North America and around 60% worldwide.[9]

In the presence of abundant megaherbivores and limited use of human-lit controlled burns, one can make several suppositions about the environment. We can presume that fires would have almost exclusively occurred as a result of lightning (or in rare cases magma extrusions).[10] Larger populations of herbivores were present to consume the grass and other fuels, and lightning is more common in the rainy season when grass is green and less combustible. In essence, fire stepped in as a substitute for the ecological services that megaherbivores once provided. This has led to ecosystems becoming fire-adapted, often at the cost of broader food web complexity and stability.

This perspective is echoed by Tim Flannery, an Australian mammalogist, who posits that this exact mechanism occurred in Australia, reducing the fire-sensitive plant populations and increasing the fire-resistant and fire-dependent plant populations. We can see that Australia's ecosystems have become reliant on regular burning—an adaptation to the absence of large herbivores—creating

---

9. Firestone, R. B. (2019, July 24). *Disappearance of Ice Age Megafauna and the Younger Dryas Impact*. Capeia. https://beta.capeia.com/planetary-science/2019/06/03/disappearance-of-ice-age-megafauna-and-the-younger-dryas-impact

10. Scott, A. C. (2018, June 1). When Did Humans Discover Fire? The Answer Depends on What You Mean By 'Discover.' *TIME*. https://time.com/5295907/discover-fire/

a suboptimal dependency for maintaining biodiversity. Properly managed cattle at high densities can help improve the situation.

From a purely theoretical standpoint, regular controlled burns run afoul of our now-established fundamental principles and are counterproductive if our goal is to minimize systemic entropy. By systemic entropy, I refer to the introduction of disorder and inefficiency into ecosystems. Controlled burns reduce opportunities for biological cycling by releasing stored energy into the atmosphere, requiring it to re-enter the food web through slower processes. However, it may sometimes be necessary to perform a 'hard reset' on the ecosystem, as chemotherapy is sometimes necessary to treat a cancerous body.

Burning would rarely, if ever, be used as a regular tool for land management in an optimized ecosystem. Fire, of both the cool and hot varieties, tends to be a blunt instrument that yields imprecise results. While a necessary tool in our current context, fire remains a stopgap in ecosystems that lack the regenerative processes of megaherbivore grazing. This is akin to periodically utilizing a pressure relief valve to prevent catastrophic failure—effective in the short term but requiring complementary efforts to manage pressure buildup sustainably.

Megaherbivores, bunched tightly and harvesting a very high percentage of the forage, perform the function of cycling and resetting landscapes far more effectively than fire. Their activity resets and revivifies without unnecessary entropy. When material is processed biologically (in this case, through fermentation), it immediately becomes food for surrounding lifeforms. When a moribund plant burns and releases CO_2 into the atmosphere, it must re-enter a plant in order to join the larger food web. This process creates an additional energy step that delays re-entry into the food web, reducing overall efficiency. Excessive burning in lieu of grazing deprives the extended food web, robbing it of the opportunity to build complexity and stability.

I would be remiss to ignore the practical considerations that make controlled burns such a large part of our toolkit in land management today. While Pleistocene-derived grazing systems offer a more ecologically aligned solution, the infrastructure, technology, and herbivore populations required to implement them at scale are currently beyond reach. Modern high-density grazing methods can approximate these ecological functions and help reduce reliance on fire in certain areas. As such, controlled burns remain a vital part of contemporary land management.

Ultimately, the current dependence on fire reflects an ecosystem's adjustment to the absence of large grazing animals. While fire can maintain biodiversity in these altered ecosystems, it remains an inefficient substitute for the biological cycling and energy flow once performed by megaherbivores. Looking forward, increased facilitation of high-density grazing practices could offer an opportunity to reduce fire dependency and restore greater ecological resilience.

HERDS AND THE MAKING OF HUMANITY

During the Pleistocene, the human brain tripled in size. At the onset of this period, our ancestor Homo Habilis emerged. Uncovered at the Olduvai Gorge in Tanzania between 1960 and 1963, Homo Habilis, nicknamed 'handy man,' was the creator of thousands of stone tools found at the site[11]. With a cranial capacity of around 500 cm^3, Habilis represents the early stages of human cognitive development. Fast forward to modern Homo Sapiens Sapiens, whose cranial capacity has expanded to around 1500 cm^3—an astonishing evolutionary leap!

It is clear that an individual's environment significantly influences development. For humanity, a long-term environment conducive to growth, safety, and stability was necessary to enable this leap in cerebral capacity. Humanity evolved in the savanna, a landscape shaped in large part by the movement of megaherbivores. These herds not only created the environment but also facilitated human migration from Africa to far-flung parts of the globe during the Pleistocene.[12]

When Giants Fell: Ecosystem Shifts

A rich body of literature demonstrates that the Pleistocene

11. Homo habilis. (2022, July 1). The Smithsonian Institution's Human Origins Program. https://humanorigins.si.edu/evidence/human-fossils/species/homo-habilis

12. Muttoni, G., Kent, D. V., Scardia, G., & Monesi, E. (2014). Migration of hominins with megaherbivores into Europe via the Danube-Po Gateway in the late Matuyama climate revolution.

was dominated by a savanna ecology. However, the disappearance of megaherbivores at the end of the Pleistocene corresponds with the shift away from this ecosystem. This environmental transition is well-documented in studies, and I will cite key examples to emphasize just how critical the megaherbivore-savanna relationship is to the core arguments presented in this book.

ASIA

"Our carbon isotope results of the extensive faunal baseline implied the ***expansion of a forest-grassland mosaic ecosystem into the high-altitude or mountainous area of Pang Mapha, up to about 600 m above present-day sea level, where the mixture of semi-evergreen and dry dipterocarp forests is typical of this elevation today***. Many types of savanna formations are still present today across MSEA, but they are mostly patchy and fragmented. This study suggests that mixed tropical forest/grasslands were more widespread and connected in MSEA during the terminal Pleistocene, as many grazing species relied exclusively on C4 grasses...

"This study reinforces the higher-latitude and altitude extension of a forest-grassland mosaic ecosystem or savanna corridor (farther north into northwestern Thailand), which facilitated the dispersal of hunter-gatherers across mountainous areas and possibly allowed for consistency in a human subsistence strategy...[13]

---

13. Suraprasit, K., Shoocongdej, R., Chintakanon, K. *et al.* Late Pleistocene

"High δ13C values from the Saleh Cave guano provide unequivocal evidence that ***relatively open and dry environments*** were present in southern Borneo during the Late Pleistocene...

"... the Saleh record demonstrates that ***closed rainforest canopy was established during the Holocene***."[14]

The passages above support the idea that savanna ecosystems were once more widespread across Asia during the Pleistocene, particularly in regions like Mainland Southeast Asia (MSEA) and southern Borneo. These mixed forest-grassland mosaics, which facilitated the movement of hunter-gatherers and supported grazing species that thrived on warm-season grasses, gradually transitioned during the Holocene into more closed forest systems, such as the rainforests of Borneo.

NORTH AMERICA

"The ***elimination of megaherbivores elsewhere in the world by human hunters at the end of the Pleistocene would have promoted reverse changes in vegetation. The conversion of the open parklike woodlands and mosaic grasslands typical of much of North America during the Pleistocene to the more uniform forests***

---

human paleoecology in the highland savanna ecosystem of mainland Southeast Asia. *Sci Rep* 11, 16756 (2021). https://doi.org/10.1038/s41598-021-96260-4

14. Wurster, C.M., Rifai, H., Zhou, B. *et al.* Savanna in equatorial Borneo during the late Pleistocene. *Sci Rep* 9, 6392 (2019). https://doi.org/10.1038/s41598-019-42670-4

> ***and prairie grasslands we find today could be a consequence***. Such habitat changes would have been detrimental to the distribution and abundance of smaller herbivores dependent upon the nutrient-rich and spatially diverse vegetation created by megaherbivore impact."[15]

This excerpt underscores the presence of a vast savanna mosaic ecosystem that once covered much of North America during the Pleistocene. The author posits that the extinction of megaherbivores by human hunters contributed to the transition from these open, diverse landscapes to the more uniform forests and prairie grasslands we observe today. While the ecological insights are valuable, I fundamentally disagree with the simplistic notion that overhunting caused megaherbivore extinction.

> The Willamette Valley[16]
>
> "The inferred dietary specializations and habitat preferences of the fauna also supports the contention that the Willamette Valley was a more open landscape in the late Pleistocene prior to ~13,000 cal BP...
>
> "... the ***timing of megafaunal decline correlates with Clovis, the onset of the***

---

15. Owen-Smith, N. (1987). Pleistocene extinctions: the pivotal role of megaherbivores. *Paleobiology, 13*(3), 351–362. doi:10.1017/S0094837300008927

16. Gilmour, D. M., Butler, V. L., O'Connor, J. E., Davis, E. B., Culleton, B. J., Kennett, D. J., & Hodgins, G. (2015). Chronology and Ecology of Late Pleistocene Megafauna in the Northern Willamette Valley, Oregon. *Quaternary Research, 83*(1), 127–136. doi:10.1016/j.yqres.2014.09.003

Younger Dryas, and increased forested conditions...

"... the timing of megafaunal decline correlates with the onset of the Younger Dryas, increased forested conditions...

"Fifth, the timing of the loss of megafauna coincides with increased forested conditions in the region."

The far western edge of North America, including the Willamette Valley, experienced a similar transition from savanna ecosystems to closed forests following the extinction of megaherbivores. As the excerpts suggest, the decline of megafauna coincided with the onset of the Younger Dryas and increased forest cover around 13,000 years ago.

We will see in the following passage describing Pleistocene conditions in modern-day Texas, this extinction not only altered the landscape but also left significant ecological niches unfilled, leading to a marked loss in biodiversity that other species have not replaced.

Texas[17]

"We found little evidence of compensation in the response of herbivores to the loss of their larger-bodied congeners. Rather, the ecological legacy of the extinction was a strikingly truncated mammal community lacking much of its former ecological complexity; the Holocene had many 'missing pieces,'

17. Smith, Felisa A., et al. "Late Pleistocene megafauna extinction leads to missing pieces of ecological space in a North American mammal community." *Proceedings of the National Academy of Sciences* 119.39 (2022): e2115015119.

each representing absent body size and isotopic niche space. ***For example, the Pleistocene community contained a rich grazer guild of mammoth and multiple horse and bison species, well-differentiated in combined body size and isotopic niche space.*** Nearly all of these taxa went extinct with only a single grazer, B. bison, occupying this isotopic niche space in the Holocene...

"With the exception of a few locations, such as African savannah ecosystems, the world has continued to lose much of its large animal biodiversity over the Holocene. Wildlife have been largely replaced with domesticated animals, and remaining natural areas are under threat. Our study suggests that even after thousands of years, ***surviving small-bodied species do not compensate for lost large-bodied ones***. Moreover, we can expect that ecological interactions between surviving species will be disrupted in the future. Thus, continued biodiversity loss will not only truncate the range of ecological function within communities but will also further reduce the complexity of natural ecosystems."

EUROPE

"... and the estimated extinction time of woolly mammoth was either at 13,830 (GRIWM) or 15,210 (PHASE), and reindeer at 11,860 (GRIWM) or 12,550 cal BP (PHASE). The population decline of the large herbivore fauna slightly preceded changes in terrestrial vegetation, and likely facilitated it

> via a reduction in the intensity of grazing and the concomitant accumulation of plant biomass."[18]

These and many other examples show that ecosystems once dominated by savannas quickly transitioned into overgrown forests, prairies, or desert landscapes following the extinction of the megaherbivores around 12,800 years ago. While we can't definitively claim that megaherbivores were the sole force behind the widespread presence of savanna ecosystems, we can confidently say that their activity was essential for maintaining these landscapes.[19]

It is clear that megaherbivores play a crucial role in preventing trees and shrubs from overtaking grasslands.[20] They also have a significant impact on arid environments. In these dry areas, where water is scarce, the primary mechanism for forage to cycle biologically throughout the year is through the digestive systems of herbivores.

While modern science struggles to directly measure the precise impact of extinct megapredators on megaherbivores, the evidence provided by contemporary ranching pioneers who employ higher animal densities offers compelling

---

18. Magyari, Enikő Katalin, et al. "Mammal extinction facilitated biome shift and human population change during the last glacial termination in East-Central Europe." *Scientific reports*12.1 (2022): 6796.

19. Pringle, Robert M., et al. "Impacts of large herbivores on terrestrial ecosystems." *Current Biology* 33.11 (2023): R584-R610.

20. Bakker, E. S., Gill, J. L., Johnson, C. N., Vera, F. W. M., Sandom, C. J., Asner, G. P., & Svenning, J. C. (2015). Combining paleo-data and modern exclosure experiments to assess the impact of megafauna extinctions on woody vegetation. *Proceedings of the National Academy of Sciences, 113*(4), 847–855. https://doi.org/10.1073/pnas.1502545112

insight. These results suggest that the ancient mechanisms—those interactions between predators and megaherbivores that once governed ecosystems—were of a vastly different scale in terms of their ecological power and functionality. Even when we push modern management systems to their limits, we're merely approximating what these ancient systems achieved effortlessly.

The herd effect—larger and denser herds—represents the most effective means for humans to manage ecosystem processes on land. This is the best approximation of the vast ecological impacts that once came from large-bodied herds. While we can't truly replace these ancient animals, we can replicate the vital effects of their presence. It is with high-density herd activity that we can begin to shift the trajectory of our planet's health. Why? Because it is both necessary and glaringly absent from most of our ecosystems today.

Herd activity is the pulse of the ecosystem—if we're searching for the most impactful lever to pull, this is it.

THE EVOLUTIONARY PSYCHOLOGY OF SAVANNAS

Savannas offered the most hospitable environment for humanity's evolution, providing both perspective—enabling us to spot predators—and refuge, allowing us to retreat from them. When herds cleared the grass, humans could finally enjoy the luxury of repose. Our nervous systems calmed, and we could gaze out across the horizon, reassured by the enhanced buffer of safety around us.

The presence of abundant herds made protein more

easily accessible to the tribe or village. As the herds passed, the insect population dwindled, their habitats disrupted annually. Meanwhile, flocks of hungry birds swarmed overhead, scavenging, while other species hunted in the disturbed grass below. With the herd's passing came a burst of new growth, as every edible plant sprouted tender and leafy. It was truly a time of plenty—all made possible by the herds' activity.

The influence of herd activity runs deep within our psyche. It is so integral to our sense of self that we replicate its effects wherever we go. Golf courses are meticulously maintained savannas with tightly grazed grass. Country estates, city parks—they all echo the same pattern.

Central Park is a prime example. Nestled in the heart of one of the most urbanized areas on Earth—where humanity's most abstract pursuits thrive—we have painstakingly recreated a savanna, maintaining the grass at just the right length. Whether large or small, every civilized space seems to have its version of parkland, unconsciously modeled after the habitat that shaped us.

Wherever possible, humans instinctively recreate savannas. It's a drive as fundamental as bees building a hive or foxes constructing a den.

Every sporting event takes place on land that mimics the severely grazed grass of the savanna, where the grass is kept short and uniform. No sport is played in tall grass. A ball only rolls or bounces on short grass or hard surfaces—both environments where control and predictability reign. Severely grazed grass creates a uniform physical environment that ensures structural fairness, much like the savanna landscape, which provided early humans with the clarity and vantage to navigate their world. In contrast, tall grass—where predators lurk—represents an environment of chaos and unpredictability. War, much like this tall grass, thrives in the disorder of the environment. While sports create a fair, level playing field to test skills, war capitalizes on exploiting unfair advantages through the breakdown of control and predictability.

This brings us to the profound connection between our evolutionary past and how we experience these environments today. The savanna did more than provide safety from predators; it also shaped our psychology and the way we interact with the world around us. In the savanna, the presence of herd animals and the surrounding landscape was a constant source of safety and order, creating the conditions for clear thinking, strategic action, and long-term survival. This enduring relationship with the landscape and the herds became embedded in our psyche. Our instincts for fairness, strategic planning, and competition—manifested in sports—are direct echoes of the conditions that once ensured our survival. Yet, these deeply ingrained traits were honed in a world of massive herds that no longer exists, leaving us to find ways to recreate and simulate the order they once facilitated.

Think of the velociraptors stalking through the tall grass in *Jurassic Park*, the Predator stalking humans in the movie *Predator*, soldiers creeping through the tall grass in *Apocalypse Now*, or Kevin Costner and several Sioux Indians slowly advancing through tall grass towards bison in *Dances with Wolves*. All of these movies employ the existing neural program of primates to evoke the fear and suspense that our ancient ancestors felt almost every day on the savannas.

Then there is music. No one attends concerts in tall grass. Can you imagine a bunch of hippies at a Phish concert twisting and dancing in waist-high grass? It would never happen, because people go to concerts (especially jam bands) to experience a state of calm nervous systems mediated by large magnitude sound frequencies. This would not be possible in tall grass, where the chaos of unpredictability takes hold. People crave the calm provided by the open, uniform space of a concert venue, akin to the cleared savanna that provided our ancestors with both refuge and perspective. It is in the controlled, safe environment—where we know the boundaries and can predict the flow—that we can fully engage with the experience. Similarly, any mother of small children will testify that she cannot relax if her child is playing in or near tall, thick grass. The unpredictability of the environment undermines her ability to fully settle into the moment, much like how the chaotic world outside the savanna once undermined humanity's sense of security and stability.

Herd activity is hidden even in our celebration and pursuit of the divine. The inside of any great cathedral or temple is filled with columns and support pillars reaching upward and outward, reminiscent of the great savanna trees from our deep past. The light filtering through stained glass windows recreates the awe and sublimity our ancient ancestors felt while resting on freshly grazed fields, surrounded by the beauty of nature, as the reds, oranges, and yellows of the setting sun passed through the branches, embodying a sense of community and anticipation for the night.

This realization struck me during a visit to the Museo Nacional Central de Arte Reina Sofia in Madrid, Spain. Amidst the masterpieces of Picasso, Dali, and countless others, I found myself drawn not only to the art but to what lay at the very heart of the museum: a courtyard that, perhaps unconsciously, resembled a savanna. The most striking feature wasn't the fountains—clear representations of water sources—or the trees scattered across the space, but a sculpture named Carmen. This monumental work by Alexander Calder—a mobile of intersecting triangles pointing skyward—stood at the center, its red and yellow pieces shifting gently in the wind.

The very concept of this courtyard as a simulated savanna—and the sculpture positioned at its heart—spoke to me in the way that art, at its best, speaks to an audience. In a museum celebrating human creativity and intellect, the most significant piece of art wasn't the paintings on the walls but this living, breathing simulation of the savanna. At its center, the Carmen sculpture rose like a spire in a church, directing our gaze upwards, with the dancing red and yellow pieces hinting at the heavenly rewards that might come from contemplation of the divine.

It felt as though this artwork wasn't just symbolizing human creativity, but echoing the ancient connection between humanity, nature, and the heavens. Standing there, I could feel the tumblers in my mind falling into place, as if the realization had been locked away until that very moment. The connection between the savanna, art, culture, and our relationship with nature clicked, unveiling a deeper truth I had never consciously recognized before: the savanna was where we found God.

HUMANS AS THE MISSING KEYSTONE

We find ourselves at a pivotal moment in history. The vast populations of megaherbivores, which once maintained the landscape, have vanished in the blink of a geological eye. Yet, much of the ecological machinery they sustained still lingers. While dramatic shifts have occurred—such as forests encroaching upon savannas or grasslands giving way to deserts—the plant and animal species that once thrived in these ecosystems remain a part of the broader ecological fabric.

This brings us to a challenging reality: humanity must now consciously harness and replicate the instinctual activities of herd animals across the planet in order to reverse the ecological shifts that threaten not just our survival, but the entire biosphere. If the presence and dominance of megaherbivores were key to the emergence and flourishing of humanity, then their disappearance—along with the ecological roles they played—may be driving a profound decline.

Planet Earth has an expectation: she relies on herds of megaherbivores to sweep across her landscapes, maintaining healthy grasslands and preventing forests from overtaking them. It is a mistake to assume that our out-of-balance ecosystems are functioning properly simply because they appear unchanged. Nature is signaling that this is not the case. The mechanisms that once governed the Earth's ecology through the heart of the Pleistocene still operate today, but they are faltering in the absence of their prime mover—herds of megaherbivores.

Herds are the engine driving Earth's terrestrial ecology in a properly functioning system. This aligns with the core principle that cattle, when managed in herds, serve as a vital eco-maintenance mechanism.

Therefore, we must ask ourselves: how can humanity recreate the migratory effect of extinct megaherbivores? First, we must identify the missing components. For our purposes, there are two essential missing elements: 1) large herds of plant-eating animals that migrated across landscapes in search of fresh forage, driven by the necessity of staying grouped up for protection coupled with the need for fresh grass, and 2) the predators that created the necessity to stay tightly bunched in the first place. The interaction between these two missing pieces is a keystone for a properly functioning landscape.

At first glance, the solution seems simple: bring back bison, and we should be able to restore ecological balance! Bison are a naturally evolved megaherbivore, and while they didn't fully go extinct, they still play a vital role in maintaining a healthy ecosystem.

However, the challenge lies in the fact that bison are wild animals, while cattle are domesticated. The planet has shifted; it's now largely dominated by human activity, with approximately 50% of the Earth's landmass affected by human influence and up to 90% altered in some way. Bison, being wild, cannot be managed with the same precision or safety as domesticated cattle.[21] Additionally, vast expanses of land now require extremely high densities of grazing animals to replicate the herd-driven impacts that megaherbivores once had. Cattle are better suited to these conditions and can be grazed at densities of up to 1 million pounds per acre. Managing bison at such densities remains a much more difficult—if not impossible—feat.

The fact that bison and cattle are so closely related they can interbreed lends weight to the idea that cattle offer an excellent functional alternative. They can be managed with greater precision, making them an effective substitute for the ecological roles that megaherbivores once filled.

However, even if we could manage bison at the density needed to restore ecological balance, it's important to note that only around 500,000 bison exist today, while approximately 1.7 billion cattle roam the earth. This means that for every bison, there are about 3,400 cattle. Given these numbers, it's mathematically unlikely that bison alone could restore the balance. We need to rely on what we have available—cattle, along with sheep and goats, albeit to a lesser degree.

If we acknowledge the crucial role that herd animals play in ecosystem health, as well as the need to slow and reverse the ongoing decline of terrestrial ecosystems, we must accept that effective management of these herds—

---

21. J. Martin. (2023, March 24). *Getting started with Bison ranching*. SDSU Extension. https://extension.sdstate.edu/getting-started-bison-ranching

through the strategic application of herd effect—is essential to restore ecological balance.

We can think of Earth's ecology like an engine, with each revolution of the planet being akin to one turn of a piston in the crankshaft. Even when an engine faces catastrophic issues, it takes thousands of revolutions for the damage to become irreversible. Similarly, one human lifetime is only a brief moment in the vast timeline of ecological change. The fact that we are witnessing rapid declines and extinctions in real-time signals that we have entered a dangerously accelerated ecological decline.

FROM MEGAHERDS TO MODERNITY: RETHINKING LIVESTOCK MANAGEMENT

"If you're not adding things back in at least 10% of the time, you're clearly not deleting enough."

- Elon Musk

To understand how we should breed and manage cattle today, we must first examine how herd animals functioned in vast prehistoric ecosystems before human intervention. During the Pleistocene (2.6 MYA – ~12,800 YBP), immense herds of mammoth, mastodon, giant bison, antelope, and even armadillos the size of golf carts migrated across landscapes in numbers that defy modern comprehension. These megaherbivores shaped their environment as they moved, acting as the primary architects of the grassland ecosystems that supported them.

These animals remained bunched for security from mega-predators such as the Saber-Toothed Cat, American Lion, Dire Wolf, the American Cheetah, and others. These, by the way, are just a selection of North American predators.

Today, Africa provides the last living example of a megaherbivore-dominated ecosystem under genuine predatory pressure, yet it now hosts only a single hypercarnivore over 100 kg—the African Lion. By contrast, during the Pleistocene, the American Lion and Cave Lion each weighed between 200 and 400 kg, and they were only part of a more extensive predator guild. Not only were there larger predators, but there were also more species of them per herbivore.[22] The evolutionary advantages of staying tightly grouped for protection in such an environment were unmistakable.

This tight grouping resulted in megaherds harvesting forage with stunning efficiency, requiring near-constant movement in search of fresh grazing. In their wake, they left what would appear, to the modern eye, as utter devastation—grasslands stripped bare, trampled earth, manure littered across the ground, and the occasional carcass feeding a flurry of scavengers. If someone unfamiliar with this process were to witness it today, they might assume the land had been permanently wrecked, a casualty of overgrazing and

22. Van Valkenburgh, B., Hayward, M. W., Ripple, W. J., Meloro, C., & Roth, V. L. (2016). The impact of large terrestrial carnivores on Pleistocene ecosystems. *Proceedings of the National Academy of Sciences, 113*(4), 862-867.

destruction. Yet, paradoxically, this apparent ruin was the key to renewal. The churned soil, fertilized by dung and debris, absorbed moisture more readily. The crushed plant material decomposed, feeding the microbial life beneath. The system had not been depleted; it had been reset—primed for an explosion of new life.

As the herds moved, the sky above them teemed with life. Massive flocks of birds followed in their wake, diving and swooping to feast on the insects stirred up by the chaos of hooves. Others rifled through the freshly dropped manure, searching for worms, eggs, and undigested seeds, scattering and breaking it apart as they fed. Below them, an army of dung beetles—unhindered by modern anthelmintics—worked tirelessly, burying and repurposing the waste into the soil. This relentless cycle of consumption, disturbance, and decomposition was not incidental but integral, ensuring that every ounce of fertility was recycled back into the earth.

The sheer scale of dung production in ancient landscapes is difficult to grasp. A single mammoth or mastodon would have dropped an 18 kg manure pile up to 15 times a day, and when multiplied across vast herds, the volume of organic material was staggering.[23] This wasn't just waste—it was an entire economy of fertility, fueling microbial life, feeding insects, and nourishing the soil. The efficiency of this system depended on animals moving in dense formations,

---

23. Foundation, T. A. (n.d.). *10 fantastic elephant facts you'll never forget!* 10 Fantastic Elephant Facts You'll Never Forget! https://blog.aspinallfoundation.org/10-fantastic-elephant-facts-youll-never-forget#:~:text=An%20adult%20elephant's%20poo%20weighs,tonnes%20of%20poo%20every%20week!

blanketing the ground with fresh manure in concentrated bursts. In such conditions, dung beetles thrived, swarming in to rapidly bury and recycle nutrients.

Today, dung beetles are in decline—not just because of modern anthelmintics, but due to the collapse of large-scale herd activity. A lone dung beetle scouring a landscape for an isolated manure pile is an unsustainable proposition. The energy required to locate and process a single pile is far greater than what the system would have offered when thousands of animals provided a continuous, predictable supply. The disappearance of high-impact grazing patterns has fractured the feedback loops that once made nutrient cycling self-sustaining.

What this demonstrates is a fundamental truth: when natural processes are intact, they create abundance. When they are broken, efficiency collapses. The plight of dung beetles serves as a microcosm of the broader challenge we face—restoring the missing links in ecological function. Cattle, when properly managed, offer one of the most effective tools to rebuild these lost relationships and reinstate the natural mechanisms of fertility and renewal.

The massive prehistoric herds that shaped ecosystems had no reliance on human intervention. If an animal struggled to calve, there was no assistance—its genetic lineage simply ended. There were no dewormers, vaccines, protein supplements, or probiotics. Survival depended solely on the ability to thrive on the landscape's natural provisions: forage, browse, and the occasional mineral lick from exposed rock faces or salt flats.

More significantly, these animals were never afforded

modern livestock's most profound, yet least acknowledged, advantage: year-round preferential grazing without predation. Preferential grazing—the ability to pick and choose the best forage without competition or pressure—is arguably the most damaging ecological disruption of the modern era. By eliminating large predators, we have created an unnatural environment where livestock are free to graze selectively, no longer driven to bunch, move, and stimulate the landscape. For centuries, domesticated herbivores have existed in an unprecedented state of ease, untethered from the pressures that once shaped their behavior and, by extension, the health of entire ecosystems.

All animals will graze selectively when given the chance. In an environment free from competition or predation, a megaherbivore has no need to stay bunched with its kind for protection. A solitary polled heifer on an open hillside is an easy meal—an enticing target that would have been quickly picked off by now-extinct dire wolves. A herd of 1,000 bison, however, moving tightly as one, presents a far greater challenge, where injury or death for a predator is just as likely as success.

Preferential grazing is not just a byproduct of modern livestock systems—it is a major ecological distortion. It disrupts biodiversity, depletes soil organic carbon, reduces water retention, and diminishes essential nutrients and minerals in the landscape. Without the natural pressures that once dictated movement, the land suffers. As our understanding of ecological function deepens, it has become clear: our role as land stewards must include actively simulating the presence of apex predators. If we fail to enforce movement and density, the entire system continues to stall, lingering in a degraded state rather than regenerating as it once did under natural herd dynamics.

The result of properly oriented herd activity was far greater harvest efficiency and significantly longer, more consistent rest periods for the land. While smaller, less migratory browsing herbivores would have continued to pick at forage between the passage of large herds, the bulk of the biomass was consumed in a single, intense grazing event. In most seasonal rainfall ecosystems, this would have occurred no more than once or twice per year. Evidence of this cycle can still be seen today on the African savanna, where large herds move in response to seasonal rainfall patterns, consuming forage in waves before leaving the land to recover.[24]

It is also important to recognize that the forage quality of that time was likely much higher than what we see today. For thousands of years, landscapes had not been subjected to mineral depletion, nutrient extraction, or unnatural grazing patterns driven by human land use. Modern rangelands, in contrast, often require external supplementation due to decades, if not centuries, of degradation. While livestock today face a very different ecological reality, the fundamental principle remains: the key to restoring these landscapes is through the intelligent use of herd behavior to replicate the missing functions of the past.

---

24. *Serengeti wildebeest migration explained with moving map.* (n.d.). Expert Africa. https://www.expertafrica.com/tanzania/info/serengeti-wildebeest-migration

Many zebras exist with a parasite load that would prove fatal to a modern horse.[25] [26] This is a beautiful example of inherent parasite resistance, shaped by evolutionary pressures we don't fully understand. It also points to symbiotic relationships that we, in our drive to naively correct nature, have unknowingly disrupted. We limit the symbiotic relationship between plants by applying herbicides. We limit symbiotic possibilities in livestock by eliminating parasites, failing to consider what role they might play in the broader system. This, in turn, wipes out dung beetles—their populations collapsing under the weight of chemical dewormers. Once you've seen dung beetles spirit a manure pile away in two days, you begin to grasp just how inefficient the modern ecosystem has become in the shadow of our conscious manipulation. And if we've lost this, what else have we lost?

Restoring balance to herbivores and their ecosystems requires a two-pronged approach—one that must be executed with both precision and restraint. First, we must select and propagate animals that are better adapted to performing their ecological role. Second, we must leverage

---

25. KRECEK, R. C., REINECKE, R. K., & MALAN, F. S. (1987). STUDIES ON THE PARASITES OF ZEBRAS. V. NEMATODES OF THE BURCHELL'S AND HARTMANN'S MOUNTAIN ZEBRAS FROM THE ETOSHA NATIONAL PARK, SOUTH WEST AFRICA/NAMIBIA. In *Onderstepoort Journal of Veterinary Research* (Vol. 54, pp. 71–78). https://repository.up.ac.za/bitstream/handle/2263/42627/14krecek1987.pdf?sequence=1&isAllowed=y

26. Salem SE, El-Ghany AMA, Hamad MH, et al. Prevalence of gastrointestinal nematodes, parasite control practices and anthelmintic resistance patterns in a working horse population in Egypt. *Equine Vet J.* 2021; 53: 339–348. https://doi.org/10.1111/evj.13325

technology, inputs, and strategic management to help them accomplish what they no longer can on their own. In other words, we must shape them from the inside and support them from the outside.

SELECTING FOR HARMONY: IMPROVING CATTLE GENETICS

If we are to return grazers to a state where they thrive under pre-Holocene conditions, we must apply selective pressures similar to those that shaped them for millennia. This means prioritizing fertility above all else—selecting for cattle that not only conceive early but also calve efficiently under real-world conditions.

The most reliable way to propagate fertility is through the sons of highly fertile cows. The ideal animal breeds at 12 to 14 months, calves at two and three years of age, and maintains good body condition without excessive supplementation. But fertility alone is not enough. For these genetics to serve their ecological function, they must develop within a system that enforces non-preferential grazing—where every mouthful is dictated by necessity rather than indulgence. While implementing non-preferential grazing may not yet be feasible across all landscapes, establishing it as the benchmark allows us to measure progress and steadily close the gap between current realities and the ecological ideal.

Non-preferential grazing is not just beneficial—it is the foundation for restoring landscapes to a state where they can once again support the natural rhythms of herd migration. Nearly a century of research, beginning with John Acocks in the 1950s, has shown that enforcing non-preferential grazing enhances ecosystem function. Yet, this practice came with an immediate challenge: cattle subjected to it often lost body condition, a reality that signaled a disconnect between modern genetics and ancestral grazing pressures.

Over the next fifty years, a handful of graziers—most notably Johann Zietsman—pioneered solutions to bridge this gap. By increasing the frequency of herd movement (often up to four times per day), offering targeted rumen supplements, and selectively breeding for cattle that thrived under these conditions, they reestablished a model of management that not only worked but mirrored the essential dynamics of ancient herd movement.[27]

For a deeper exploration of this approach, Johann Zietsman's *Man, Cattle, and Veld* remains an essential guide.

Living Lightly: Reducing External Inputs

Ruminants are not, and never will be, hind-gut fermenters. Their digestive system simply does not allow them to thrive on low-quality forage alone. This fundamental difference helps explain why hind-gut fermenters—such as elephants, mastodons, and mammoths—were able to reach immense

27. Zietsman, J. (2014). *Man, Cattle and Veld.* BEEFpower LLC.

sizes, whereas ruminants rarely exceed 1,200 lbs (550 kg) in a natural setting.[28] [29]

There are exceptions through time, particularly among certain species of bison and moose, but these cases are geographically specific. Large ruminants tend to flourish in regions dominated by high-quality, cool-season grasses. These grasses provide more protein and less fiber, enabling greater weight gain without excessive digestive heat production or non-productive digestive activity. High-fiber forages, on the other hand, present a limiting factor: they generate more internal heat during digestion, making them unsuitable for supporting massive body sizes in warmer climates. This is why, in tropical and subtropical regions, native cattle breeds remain small-framed—some as small as 300 kg. Large-framed, poorly adapted cattle struggle in these environments, often spending more time seeking shade or standing in water to cool off rather than grazing efficiently.

Regardless of climate or geography, landscapes still require low-quality forages to be grazed and cycled through herbivore digestion to maintain ecological function. This underscores the critical role once played by now-extinct hindgut fermenters, whose absence has left a void in forage processing. The question is not whether these high-fiber, stem-heavy plants should be consumed, but how to ensure

---

28. Croitor, Roman, and J. Brugal. "New insights concerning Early Pleistocene cervids and bovids in Europe: dispersal and correlation." *Courier-Forschungsinstitut Senckenberg* 259 (2007): 47.

29. All About Bison. (2023, January 18). *Ancient Bison* -. https://allaboutbison.com/ancient-bison/

they are. Since ruminants cannot process them with the same efficiency as their prehistoric counterparts, we must bridge the gap.

The best way to achieve this is twofold: first, by selecting for cattle that possess inherent fertility and adaptability—traits that reflect functional environmental fit. Second, by providing strategic protein supplementation, which fuels rumen microbes and enables cattle to better digest the fibrous material. In essence, this helps ruminants mimic the role of hindgut fermenters, allowing them to cycle tough forage that would otherwise stagnate in the system.

No amount of protein supplementation will overcome the fundamental reality of grazing behavior: cattle, like all herbivores, will choose the most palatable forage available. If given the option, they will avoid coarse, stemmy plants in favor of softer, nutrient-dense regrowth. This is why supplementation alone is insufficient—we must also enforce non-selective grazing to ensure these lower-quality forages are consumed.

When cattle are grouped tightly, competition dictates behavior. They instinctively recognize that hesitation means losing out, either to a competitor's appetite or to the inevitable fouling of forage by manure. This urgency forces them to consume what is available rather than holding out for something better. By enforcing density and movement, we guide cattle toward the ecological role they evolved to play, compelling them to cycle even the least desirable forage back into the system.

Routine deworming has become a crutch in modern livestock systems, conditioning herds to rely on chemical intervention rather than developing natural resilience. Some progressive graziers, myself included, have experimented with abrupt withdrawal, and while it has yielded success in some cases, a more measured approach is likely to produce better long-term outcomes.

Parasite resistance isn't built overnight. Expecting cattle accustomed to regular deworming to suddenly fend for themselves is unrealistic and, in many cases, counterproductive. A more effective strategy is gradual withdrawal—spacing out treatments over time and ensuring that successive generations are selected for inherent resistance. By shifting the focus from chemical dependency to genetic adaptation, we can cultivate a herd that thrives without external inputs, strengthening both ecological function and economic sustainability.

Inputs should be used sparingly and strategically—only in ways that enable the herd to fulfill its ecological role while maintaining economic viability. Every intervention should be weighed against its long-term impact, ensuring that short-term gains do not come at the expense of ecological resilience.

The Tail Wagging the Cow

It is no accident that beef production has gone unmentioned throughout this discussion. We do not graze our breeding herd with beef quality in mind, nor do we select cattle for the sake of producing a "premium" beef product. Instead, our primary goal must be ecological restoration and maintenance. Only once that foundation is firmly established can we consider beef production as a secondary outcome—never as the driving force. To allow market preferences for marbling and tenderness to dictate our grazing strategy would be to let the tail wag the dog.

Before we can even begin to discuss beef production, we must first ask: what defines a truly beneficial beef outcome? Modern consumers, particularly urban populations, have been conditioned to believe that tenderness and marbling are the sole markers of quality. While these attributes make for a more pleasant eating experience, there is a vast difference between marbling achieved through overfeeding high-energy feeds in feedlots and marbling that develops naturally in well-adapted, pasture-raised cattle. The former prioritizes rapid fattening at the expense of ecological health, while the latter yields beef that is not only more flavorful but also more nutrient-dense.

If we allow industrial definitions of quality to dictate our management practices, we will sacrifice long-term sustainability for short-term gains. But if we adhere to the fundamental principle that cattle exist as an ecological maintenance force, we will achieve a far greater outcome—landscapes that are steadily improving, resilient grazing systems, and, as a byproduct, an abundance of high-quality beef.

If we are to reverse the ecological decline, we must do more than just recognize the role of herds—we must actively elevate them as the indispensable ecological force they are. But this shift is impossible so long as cattle remain trapped in the narrow framework of a commodity, valued only for their meat rather than their function in maintaining the land.

Up to this point, we have explored the deep historical, psychological, and ecological connections between humanity and herd animals—how they shaped the land and, in turn, shaped us. But understanding this relationship is only the foundation.

Now, we must turn to the mechanics of grazing itself: how herd movement interacts with thermodynamics, how energy flows through trophic systems, and how the right management decisions can transform landscapes. By examining the interplay of fertility, infrastructure efficiency, and resource cycling, we will see how properly managed herds not only sustain themselves but serve as the engine of a thriving ecosystem.

III. HARMONY
THE PHYSICS OF BALANCE

We can't force energy to multiply—only channel and optimize its flow through thoughtful management. By design, a system rooted in voluntary participation taps into natural energy efficiencies. A better system means more energy becomes available, accessed through efficient transmission mechanisms.

Energy, by its nature, always spreads out and dissipates unless carefully managed. The history of ecological evolution is the story of optimizing energy flow. When we harness this principle, we concentrate energy in ways that foster growth and improve ecosystems.

Voluntary systems align with nature's immutable laws, reducing waste and inefficiency. In contrast, compulsory systems expend excess energy trying to force outcomes—often with diminishing returns. True sustainability lies in working with, not against, the inherent energy dynamics of life. In the following sections, we will explore in more detail how efficiency can be properly framed by examining voluntary systems and the implications of thermodynamics in herd systems.

Harmony or Discord: Voluntary vs Compulsory Systems

When two systems are pitted head-to-head: the first being a bottom-up system defined by voluntary participation, and another top-down system characterized by compulsion, the voluntary system will always win over a meaningful time horizon, and for a variety of reasons. One simple reason is that the compulsory system will waste energy enforcing an outcome. This leaves less energy available for desired outcomes.

Voluntary systems are also characterized by a larger quantity and quality of information flow whereas compulsory systems tend to suffer from the constraints of enforced information pathways.[30] Voluntary systems also produce a larger matrix of interactions by the various parts of a system.[31] This inevitably results in a more efficient transfer of energy and information, facilitating a more efficient mechanism overall. Thus, the voluntary system will always be more efficient, and the compulsory system will fail (and possibly result in the death of all participants) over any meaningful time horizon.[32]

---

30. Gonzalez, Aldo and Benitez, Daniel, Optimal Pre-Merger Notification Mechanisms - Incentives and Efficiency of Mandatory and Voluntary Schemes (May 1, 2009). World Bank Policy Research Working Paper No. 4936, Available at SSRN: https://ssrn.com/abstract=1407954

31. Hauert, Christoph, and György Szabo. "Prisoner's dilemma and public goods games in different geometries: compulsory versus voluntary interactions." *Complexity* 8.4 (2003): 31-38.

32. Hauert, Christoph, and György Szabó. "Game theory and physics." *American Journal of Physics* 73.5 (2005): 405-414.

Modern conventional agriculture and cattle breeding is characterized by using inputs (energy) to force outcomes: preferential grazing, insufficient recovery periods, excessive supplementation with hay and grain, deworming, and unnatural calving seasons all contribute to this compulsory system.

Energy in Motion: Herds and Thermodynamics

A herd of cattle—the prime movers in our ranchland ecosystem—is fundamentally a definable thermodynamic system. By thinking of our prime-moving herds as a thermodynamic system, we can set up the system to operate as close to a "voluntary" state as possible. It follows, therefore, that by establishing a "voluntary" relationship between cattle and the landscape, all other transient elements of the larger landscape system will gravitate into harmony with the central function—migratory herbivores.

It might be helpful to ask ourselves, "What characterizes a successful thermodynamic system?" One key indicator of a successful biosystem is sustainable iteration. Therefore, it must not waste energy unwisely. It must also avoid excessive thriftiness with energy because a central systemic element has, by definition, the capacity to starve the rest of the ecology by withholding too much energy. We see this in overgrown forests today. The migratory herds have been removed. This makes the trees and shrubs the central systemic element, and they simply hold onto all the energy at the expense of the larger carbon cycle. A "prime-mover," therefore, must maintain and reproduce itself while adequately feeding surrounding systems. It should be mentioned, however, that the threat of a herd wasting energy inappropriately is far greater than hoarding too much.

A successful and prudent biological system must therefore exist in what I will call a "zone of proximal entropy"—neither shedding nor hoarding too much energy.

The cattle world as it currently stands is characterized by massive unnecessary entropy as a result of its discontinuity with herd animals' properly oriented pre-Holocene state. This is due to both ignorance of the pre-Holocene state, the willful blindness of measuring the wrong things based on false assumptions, and the ego inflation of perfecting unnecessary, even counterproductive, activities.

RETHINKING EFFICIENCY IN GRAZING SYSTEMS

One of the most misleading metrics in modern cattle production is Feed Conversion Efficiency (FCE). The industry promotes FCE as an essential indicator of success, yet a deeper examination reveals that it is fundamentally flawed.

The logic behind FCE is seemingly straightforward: maximizing the ratio of live weight gain to feed consumed should equate to greater efficiency. If the sole purpose of cattle were to produce protein, this argument might hold. However, when we recognize that herds are not just protein factories but also critical ecological agents, FCE falls apart as a guiding principle.

By prioritizing weight gain over ecological function,

we select for animals that may perform well in artificial conditions but fail to serve their fundamental role within a healthy grazing system. This oversight highlights the danger of measuring success based on a narrow, commodity-driven perspective rather than a systems-level understanding of ecology.

If grazers are the primary functionaries of a grazing ecology, then the key measure of their success is their ability to sustain themselves across generations. The most reliable indicator of this is not sheer weight gain, but high functional fertility—the ability to conceive, carry, and raise offspring under conditions that mimic their ancestral environment. These conditions are defined by high-density, non-preferential grazing, where competition ensures that only the most well-adapted animals thrive.

If fertility is the benchmark for sustainability, then we must ask: does selecting for feed conversion efficiency improve practical fertility? The answer is no.

Practical fertility is tied directly to body condition. The ability to maintain good body condition under a non-preferential grazing regime depends on how efficiently an animal converts forage into fat. This requires a genetic predisposition toward depositing a higher ratio of adipose tissue (fat) to lean muscle and water. A post-pubescent animal typically gains weight in one of two ways: by storing either fat or protein-dense lean meat and water. Every animal, of course, exhibits some combination of both, but the balance between them has significant ecological implications. Fat requires two to three times more energy to deposit than lean meat, but it also functions as a critical buffer against environmental stress.[33]

Since feed conversion efficiency measures the ratio of kilograms of feed consumed to kilograms of weight gained, it inherently favors animals that deposit lean muscle more efficiently. This might seem advantageous at first glance, but in a real-world grazing system, the opposite is true. Practical fertility depends on the ability to store energy as fat, withstand environmental pressures, carry a pregnancy to term, and reconceive without excessive inputs. An animal selected purely for feed efficiency—prioritizing rapid lean muscle gain—will struggle in the long run. While a cow that gains weight more easily in fat may require more energy upfront, she will have far greater resilience when conditions deteriorate. When survival depends on stored energy, the advantage is clear. If I were stranded on a desert island, I'd rather have a tub of lard than a bag of carrots.

Consider the following analogy:

A fuel-efficient 4-cylinder sedan and a diesel pickup are driving on a flat road. If the goal is to travel the greatest distance using the least amount of fuel, the sedan appears to be the superior choice. But what happens when both vehicles must pull a heavy trailer up a steep hill? The sedan, despite its efficiency, may not have enough power

---

33. Tedeschi, Luis O. "Relationships of retained energy and retained protein that influence the determination of cattle requirements of energy and protein using the California Net Energy System." *Translational Animal Science* 3.3 (2019): 1029-1039.

to complete the task, whereas the diesel truck—designed for sustained workload—has the reserves to make the climb.

While this comparison is exaggerated, the same principle applies to cattle selection. The difference between animals that prioritize fat storage and those that prioritize lean muscle deposition may seem minor in a single generation. But across a herd—and over time—these subtle genetic advantages define whether a system is resilient or vulnerable. A cow's ability to maintain condition in times of stress determines both her reproductive success and the long-term sustainability of the operation.

Feed Conversion Efficiency is a textbook case of how flawed assumptions lead to misguided selection. If we frame the problem correctly from the outset, our decisions align with reality, and success compounds over time. But when we start with faulty assumptions—like prioritizing feed efficiency over ecological function—the results may seem promising in the short term but ultimately lead to systemic failures. By the time those failures become apparent, the financial and operational investments may be too deep to reverse course without serious consequences.

Take, for instance, the relationship between FCE and skeletal structure. Cattle with high FCE scores tend to have a lower flesh-to-bone ratio, often displaying large, coarse frames with excessive bone mass. Meanwhile, animals with lower FCE scores are typically finer boned, with a significantly higher flesh-to-bone ratio—traits that correlate strongly with fertility, resilience, and long-term productivity in a properly managed grazing system.

From the perspective of an optimized energy system, an

animal with excessive skeletal mass is inefficient. It diverts resources toward structural maintenance rather than toward reproduction and ecological function. The most valuable animals are those that efficiently convert energy into body condition and fertility rather than excessive bone growth. These animals tend to be finer-boned, reach sexual maturity quickly, and maintain their condition with minimal inputs. If an organism is allocating too many resources to skeletal mass rather than reproductive potential, it is less effective at both sustaining itself and contributing to the broader system.

It's also crucial to understand that as a cow doubles in size, its feed intake does not double—it only increases by about 67%. This follows Kleiber's Law, named after Swiss scientist Max Kleiber, who demonstrated that metabolic rates scale at roughly 0.75x an animal's mass. This means that while a larger cow consumes more overall, its efficiency relative to its body size decreases, making smaller, more energy-efficient cattle superior in a regenerative grazing system.[34]

A smaller cow is more efficient at cycling forage through her body each day—a fundamental ecological function. Because her maintenance requirements are lower, a greater proportion of her intake is available for growth, reproduction, and overall resilience. This gives her a competitive advantage in dynamic grazing systems where energy efficiency is paramount.

---

34. Kleiber, Max. "Body size and metabolic rate." *Physiological reviews* 27.4 (1947): 511-541.

When we analyze cattle through the lens of thermodynamics, each individual animal functions as a biological system organized for sustained energy transfer. One of the primary ways a cow reduces unnecessary energy loss (entropy) is through reproduction—producing more organized biological units that perpetuate the system. Fertility, then, is not just a metric of productivity but a critical mechanism for maintaining ecological balance and systemic efficiency.

From this perspective, the most valuable cow is not simply the largest or fastest-growing but the one that produces the most calves throughout her lifespan while maintaining the highest weaning weight relative to her body size. Crucially, she must do so within a high-density, non-preferential grazing system and with minimal external inputs.

Herds that thrive under these conditions perpetuate "sustained biological organization"—a state where cattle utilize naturally available resources rather than relying on costly, energy-intensive external inputs. This reduces unnecessary entropy, allowing the system to function with greater stability and long-term efficiency.

Extending plant recovery periods maximizes the sustained biological organization of the landscape. When plants are given sufficient time to capture sunlight and convert it into usable energy for themselves and soil microbiota, they contribute to a more resilient ecological system. Under a high-density, non-selective grazing system, cattle harvest a much greater proportion of available forage compared to rotational or set-stocking systems. This forces them to progress more slowly across the landscape, granting each grazed area an extended recovery period.

This prolonged rest cycle offers benefits far beyond soil health. It enhances the land's drought resilience by increasing its ability to retain moisture and recover from dry spells. A greater drought buffer also provides operators with more flexibility in making critical management decisions—such as adjusting stocking rates—without being forced into reactive destocking.

In these high-density systems, each small paddock experiences an intense, concentrated burst of grazing activity. Cattle harvest available forage with high efficiency, distributing manure and urine evenly while trampling leftover vegetation into the soil. This process accelerates nutrient cycling and fosters improved seed-to-soil contact, setting the stage for healthier regrowth.

Please note: This book is not intended as a comprehensive treatise on grazing management. Each operation must determine how best to apply these principles within the realities of its own context—balancing ecological restoration with the practical necessity of maintaining a profitable enterprise.

Root exudation plays a critical role in sustaining biological organization. These exudates—organic compounds secreted by plant roots—fuel microbial activity in the soil, forming the foundation of a thriving underground ecosystem. When plants are allowed sufficient recovery time, they develop deeper, more robust root systems. A larger root mass produces greater exudates, nourishing a wider range of soil microbes. As these microbes complete their life cycles, their decomposed bodies add organic matter to the soil, enriching its structure and fertility.

As soil organic matter accumulates, an increasing fraction remains stored in the subsoil for extended periods, a process known as "recalcitrant carbon" formation. This stable carbon matrix enhances soil resilience, supporting above-ground ecology for decades. Notably, the decomposition rate of soil organic matter slows over time—most carbon cycles back into the atmosphere within the first year after deposition, while approximately 10% remains stored in the soil after a decade.[35]

A high-density, non-preferential grazing system stands in stark contrast to conventional rotational grazing, which is often structured around preferential grazing—an inherently extractive process. In conventional rotational grazing, cattle are expected to consume only a fraction of each plant, theoretically leaving behind enough leaf area to promote rapid regrowth. In practice, however, this goal is rarely achieved. Cattle do not graze evenly; instead, they selectively consume the most palatable plants while avoiding less desirable species. Over time, this leads to a landscape dominated by unpalatable, lower-value vegetation.

Selective grazing also undermines the ecological processes that shaped savanna ecosystems. Historically, large herbivore herds moved in dense formations,

---

35. Y. S. Feng, Fundamental considerations of soil organic carbon dynamics: a new theoretical framework. *Soil Sci.* **2009**, *174*, 467. doi:10.1097/SS.0B013E3181BB0E87

consuming available forage in its entirety before moving on. This intense, non-selective grazing pressure, followed by extended rest periods, allowed landscapes to regenerate. By contrast, preferential grazing distorts this natural cycle, accelerating plant species imbalance and diminishing overall forage quality.

Conventional rotational grazing inherently sacrifices harvest efficiency. Since cattle are not required to consume all available forage evenly, they preferentially graze, forcing operators to rotate them more frequently. However, when livestock return to a previously grazed paddock, the most palatable plants—those heavily grazed in the previous rotation—often have not had adequate time to recover, leading to overgrazing. Simultaneously, the less palatable plants, which were ignored before, have matured further, making them even less desirable. This creates an ever-worsening imbalance—a landscape where certain plants are chronically overgrazed, while others become increasingly dominant and unpalatable.

To mitigate this imbalance, conventional operations rely on external interventions such as burning, mowing, or fertilization—often employing all three. Yet, these practices merely address symptoms rather than the root issue. By allowing undesirable species to proliferate unchecked, we perpetuate a cycle where the most ecologically and nutritionally valuable plants are systematically suppressed. Over time, the pasture becomes locked in an early succession state, where opportunistic, low-value plants dominate at the expense of biodiversity and soil health.

Early succession plants are the first to colonize a

disturbed landscape, thriving in conditions where soil health is poor and competition is minimal. In the absence of proper grazing dynamics, these plants can dominate—not because they create a stable system, but because they are well-suited to degraded conditions. A properly functioning ecosystem, however, trends toward greater complexity, where plant communities develop deeper root systems, higher biomass productivity, and increased biodiversity. Without the pressures of herd activity cycling nutrients and shaping plant competition, the land remains locked in an early-succession state—prone to stagnation rather than progress.

Rather than managing pastures through constant external intervention, the focus should be on optimizing energy flow through the ecosystem itself. This requires an understanding of trophic flow—the movement of energy and nutrients through the food web—and how grazing animals serve as the primary drivers of this process.

ENERGY ACROSS ECOSYSTEMS: THE TROPHIC FLOW

Leaf-to-Stem and Meat-to-Bone Ratios

Natural ecosystems operate as vast networks of energy exchange, where life moves through trophic levels from primary producers to apex predators. Within grazing ecosystems, two key indicators—leaf-to-stem ratio in plants and meat-to-bone ratio in herbivores—offer profound insight into both ecological functionality and cattle ranching efficiency.

A high leaf-to-stem ratio reflects a forage plant's ability to allocate more of its biomass to nutrient-dense, digestible leaf material rather than fibrous, structural stem. Likewise, a high meat-to-bone ratio in grazing animals signifies an efficient use of resources, favoring muscle growth over excessive skeletal investment. These ratios are not merely abstract measurements; they serve as tangible metrics that connect land health with livestock productivity. Their relevance to both ecosystem function and ranching operations lends further weight to their importance, affirming that their role in land management is built on a solid ecological foundation.

In both human societies and ecosystems, an optimized infrastructure is one that supports the greatest possible value with the least waste. In grazing systems, this translates to a well-structured framework of stems in plants and bones in animals, which should serve as efficient scaffolding for the storage and transfer of energy. The goal is to minimize unnecessary energy loss while maximizing functional output.

From this perspective, a well-managed grazing ecosystem is one that optimizes its infrastructure to enhance the storage and transfer of energy across trophic levels. This process is inherently self-regulating—ecosystems structured in accordance with these principles naturally maximize their own productive potential.

Understanding this infrastructure-value relationship reinforces the need to manage grazing systems in a way that enhances efficiency rather than disrupts it. If we can align our management practices with nature's inherent logic, we can facilitate the greatest possible energy capture and conversion, improving both land resilience and livestock productivity.

When a system is structured to optimize energy flow with minimal waste, both nature and human enterprises benefit. Throughout history, both evolution and human innovation have sought to refine systems by reducing inefficiencies while maximizing productive output. Yet despite this, many modern land management practices remain inefficient—not because better methods don't exist, but because the knowledge, technology, and industry-wide will to implement them have only recently emerged. While the adoption of improved grazing management has been slow relative to its potential, momentum is building. More producers are recognizing the benefits of aligning grazing practices with ecological principles, driving a shift toward more regenerative systems.

The Anatomy of Abundance: Leaf vs. Stem and Meat vs. Bone

A field of grass functions much like an array of solar panels, designed to capture and convert energy. The efficiency of this process depends on how well energy is allocated between structural support and productive function. Some energy must inevitably be used to maintain infrastructure—holding the plant upright, transporting nutrients, or sustaining root networks. However, excess energy allocated to unnecessary structural components reduces the system's overall efficiency. The same principle applies to grazing animals: an overbuilt skeletal frame diverts energy away from productive functions like muscle development and fertility. In both cases, an imbalance results in wasted energy that could otherwise contribute to the broader ecological and economic system.

Plants with a high leaf-to-stem ratio are more energy efficient and provide greater nutritional value per bite. The leaf of a Timothy hay plant, for instance, has 12–13% higher digestibility[36] than its stem.[37] Observations from Jaime Elizondo, one of my mentors, have shown that in Bermuda grass pastures subjected to conventional rotational grazing, the leaf-to-stem ratio can be as low as 20%, while pastures managed with high harvest efficiency and extended rest periods can reach up to 65% leaf. This difference doesn't just improve digestibility by over 5%; it drastically enhances photosynthetic efficiency. Because leaf area generates three to four times the photosynthetic activity of stem, an optimized pasture with a higher leaf ratio can produce up to 75% more total photosynthesis than a conventionally grazed counterpart.[38]

However, the optimal balance of leaf-to-stem ratio varies depending on environmental conditions. In cool, dry environments, plants can allocate more energy toward leaf production. In contrast, warm, humid climates

---

36. The measure of how well a food source is absorbed by the body

37. Bélanger, G., and R. E. McQueen. "Leaf and stem nutritive value of timothy grown with varying N nutrition in spring and summer." *Canadian journal of plant science* 79.2 (1999): 223-229.

38. Tokarz, Krzysztof M., et al. "Stem photosynthesis—A key element of grass pea (Lathyrus sativus L.) acclimatisation to salinity." *International Journal of Molecular Sciences* 22.2 (2021): 685.

necessitate greater investment in fibrous infrastructure (stem) to mitigate nutrient leaching and prevent excessive volatilization.

By directing more energy into leaf production and maximizing root exudates that fuel soil microbiota, we enhance both above-ground biomass and below-ground ecological function. This aligns with the fundamental principle of reducing entropy within biological systems—optimizing energy flow for maximum ecological and economic resilience.

A closer look at grazer biomass reveals that an optimized meat-to-bone ratio does more than improve energy storage—it also increases the total herbivore biomass a given landscape can support. Less energy wasted on maintaining excess skeletal structure means more energy available for muscle development, reproduction, and ecosystem contribution. The result is a more efficient conversion of available resources into productive biological output.

Beyond efficiency, a high meat-to-bone ratio directly impacts survival. Herbivores with proportionally more muscle and less bone are better suited for movement, competition, and escape. Whether it's two bulls clashing for dominance or a mother defending her calf, the ability to respond quickly and powerfully is critical. In this way, a superior meat-to-bone ratio reflects not just efficient energy use but a form of evolutionary resilience—favoring animals that are both more physically capable and better adapted to their environment.

Optimizing Meat-to-Bone Ratio

There are two approaches to improving the meat-to-bone ratio: one rooted in short-term data collection and another aligned with long-term ecological function. The short-sighted approach relies on carcass data from slaughtered animals, tracing traits back to their lineage and making selection decisions accordingly. While this method has its uses, it falls into the trap of trait-chasing—an approach that often leads to unintended consequences and narrow genetic bottlenecks.

The correct approach, instead, is to focus on practical fertility. As we have already explored, a superior meat-to-bone ratio is an inherent trait of cattle displaying high fertility and adaptation to their environment. The best way to select for this trait is not by targeting it directly, but by prioritizing the most fertile cows—those that breed early, calve efficiently, and maintain good body condition in a high-density, non-preferential grazing system. These cows will typically be smaller-framed (shorter and heavier relative to height) and produce sons that should be ranked at 12 months based on their kg/cm height ratio.

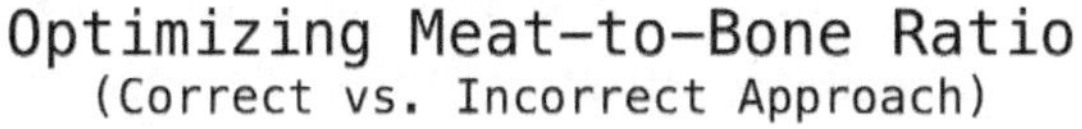

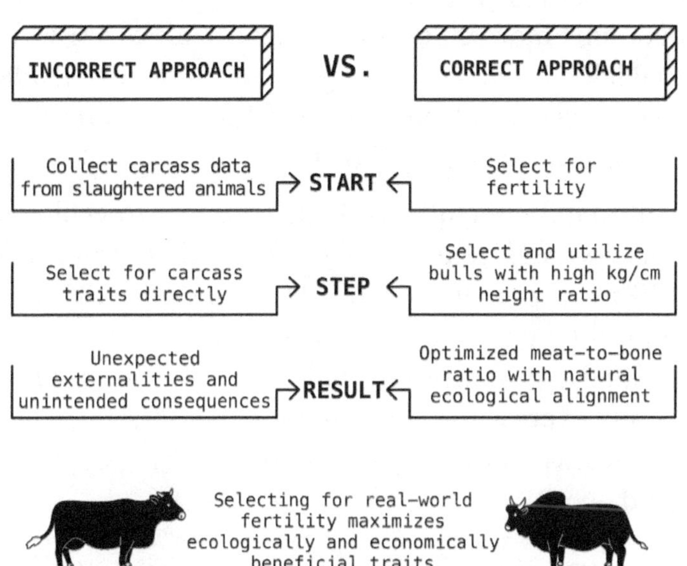

Both Johann Zietsman and Jaime Elizondo have done exceptional work in refining bull selection strategies to maximize fertility and functional efficiency. Their methodologies, which emphasize early maturity and hormonal balance, provide invaluable insights into selecting bulls that thrive in real-world grazing conditions. By focusing on inherent fertility rather than isolated production traits, they have demonstrated how proper selection can align with both ecological function and profitability.

Importantly, selecting the right bulls is the fastest and most effective way to improve adapted genetics within a herd. While culling undesirable females is a necessary practice, prioritizing superior bulls accelerates genetic progress by spreading desirable traits across multiple generations more efficiently. Their teachings are widely available both online and in print and should be studied by anyone serious about breeding for long-term resilience and regenerative grazing success.

Ultimately, fertility is the master key to ecological adaptation and genetic progress. Meat-to-bone ratio, just like every other functionally significant trait, is best improved by pursuing fertility—not by chasing traits in isolation. A properly selected, highly fertile herd will naturally express the characteristics necessary for long-term success, both for the land and for the people who depend on it.

Optimizing Leaf-to-Stem Ratio

Non-selective grazing is the key factor in maximizing the leaf-to-stem ratio. When a plant is grazed down to the crown—contrary to conventional 'regenerative' wisdom—the regrowth is disproportionately leaf-dominant. In contrast, when grazing is limited to the top half or third of the plant, a higher percentage of the remaining structure is stem. Since leaf area produces three to four times more photosynthetic activity than stem, and stems respire at quadruple the rate of leaves, the advantage of maximizing leaf growth becomes clear. Just as animals must balance energy intake and expenditure, plants must balance photosynthesis and respiration. Energy lost through unnecessary respiration—akin to metabolic inefficiency in livestock—is energy unavailable for growth, root exudation, or reproduction.

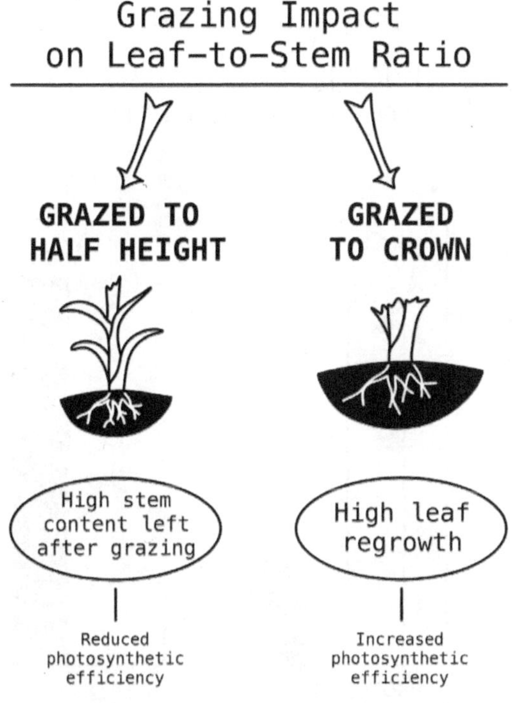

Think of the plant as an economic system. Leaves are the revenue-generating sector, while stems represent overhead costs. If we leave behind excessive stem, we're burdening the plant with unnecessary expenses while capping its income potential. Given the choice, cattle instinctively select leaves over stems because leaves contain more energy and are far more digestible. When a plant is grazed down to the crown, it prioritizes the rapid regrowth of leaves, ensuring a more energy-efficient recovery. Scaled across an entire landscape, optimizing leaf-to-stem ratios through non-selective grazing leads to a far more productive and resilient pasture system.

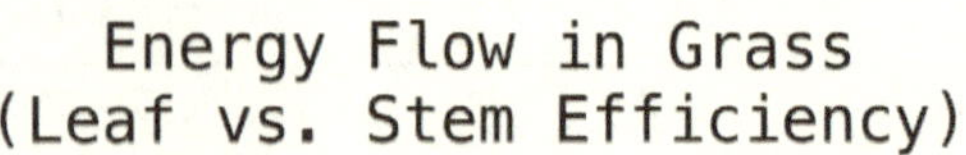

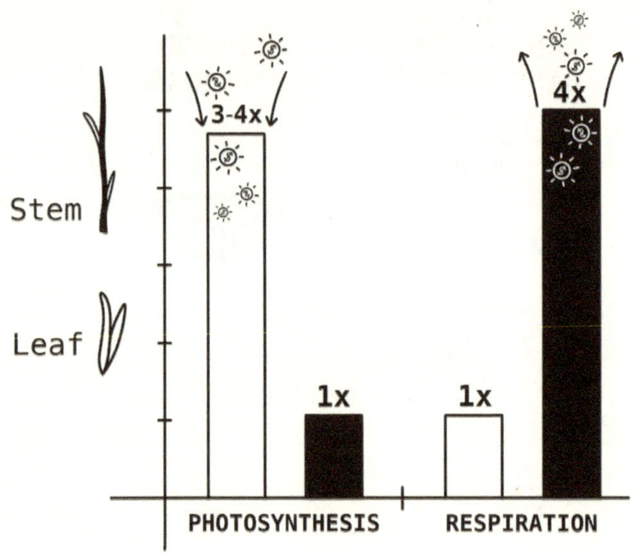

Leaf-to-stem and meat-to-bone ratios serve as key indicators of how efficiently a system converts resources into value. In both plants and animals, minimizing the infrastructure required to support productive output results in greater ecological and economic efficiency. Fertility is the nexus where these efficiencies converge. A cow with a superior meat-to-bone ratio produces more usable flesh with less structural overhead. A cow with a higher fat-to-lean-meat ratio has greater energy reserves, making her more resilient to drought, more likely to conceive, and better equipped to sustain a pregnancy under variable conditions. A cow with a shorter intercalving period spends a greater percentage of her lifespan contributing to the herd's productivity. Each of these traits reflects an optimized system where biological efficiency translates directly into ecological function.

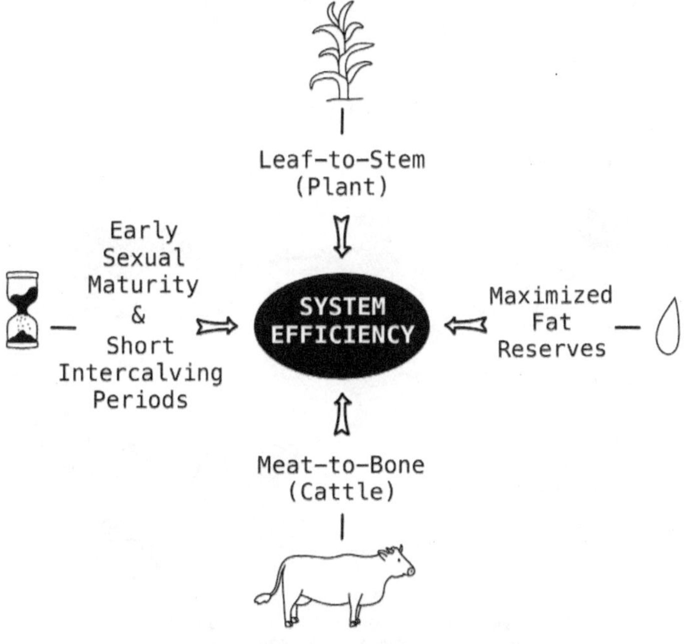

Value-to-infrastructure ratios signal productivity and ecological alignment.

By prioritizing real-world fertility, we inherently select for animals that maximize value relative to infrastructure—

traits that are essential for maintaining high-density, non-selective grazing systems. This is the key to restoring degraded landscapes while keeping operations profitable.

At its core, this entire approach rests on a simple principle: optimizing energy flows within biological systems yields exponential benefits. By allowing energy to circulate efficiently through plants, soil, and livestock, we can harness natural processes rather than fighting against them. When the system is properly aligned, nature does the heavy lifting, and we simply serve as its stewards.

Energy Flow Across the Ecosystem

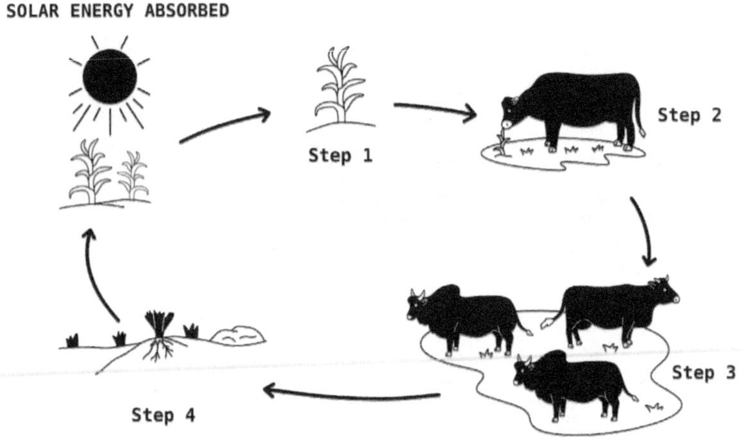

Efficient leaf-to-stem ratios and meat-to-bone ratios optimize the flow of energy across the system, reduce entropy, and increase productivity.

THE FRAMEWORK OF REGENERATION: WATER AND FENCES

Migratory herbivores functioned as nature's original irrigation systems. Without intervention, water follows gravity, accumulating in low-lying areas while leaving vast portions of the landscape dry. But the movement of large herds redistributed water across entire ecosystems.

Picture the hydrological impact of 100,000 bison drinking from a stream and then, over the course of a day, depositing that water back onto the land. A single 1,000 lb bison urinating delivers the equivalent of 1.5 inches (37.5mm) of rainfall in a concentrated area—except this isn't just water. It's a biologically rich infusion of nitrogen and other essential nutrients. The scale of this natural irrigation system is difficult to overstate.

In contrast, modern rotational or set stocking grazing schemes create artificial pressure points where livestock congregate near water sources. The result? Overgrazed, over-impacted, and overfertilized zones near water points, while outlying areas remain undergrazed, underutilized, and underfertilized.

The solution is straightforward: improve water and fencing infrastructure. A well-planned distribution of water sources ensures a more even spread of grazing, impact, and natural fertilization. Just as schools install water fountains and restrooms at strategic intervals, landscapes thrive when water and grazing pressure are balanced through thoughtful infrastructure.

Fencing infrastructure does not need to be excessive or restrictive. In most cases, high-density grazing with cattle can be accomplished with a single strand of electrified high-tensile wire. This approach is not only more cost-effective and easier to manage than conventional multi-strand barbed wire but also significantly more wildlife-friendly.

Since Pleistocene predators no longer shape herd movements as they once did, it is now our responsibility to enforce the migration effect. Electric fencing—when used intelligently—serves as a modern substitute, ensuring that grazing pressure is applied and distributed in a way that mimics natural cycles. However, other technologies, such as virtual fencing collars, are gaining in popularity and may prove to be a meaningful alternative to physical barriers in certain contexts. These systems use GPS and auditory cues to guide livestock movement, offering even greater flexibility in managing grazing pressure while further reducing impact on wildlife corridors.

Fortunately, a wealth of knowledge exists on designing and constructing fencing and water infrastructure to maximize ecological impact and operational efficiency. Investing in migratory technology and water distribution systems is among the most valuable steps humanity can take toward large-scale ecological restoration. These principles are not just a key to revitalizing our landscapes—they are a cornerstone of sustainable life, both on this planet and wherever else we may one day inhabit.

The mechanics of grazing offer us the tools and understanding, but it is the stories—of life, death, and an understanding of their inseparability—that offer meaning.

In order to develop a deeper relationship with the physical realities of grazing, let us also journey into the narratives that belie the ancient partnership of humans and herds.

IV. THE GARDEN

LIFE, DEATH, AND THE POWER OF CREATION

"In any compromise between food and poison, it is only death that can win. In any compromise between good and evil, it is only evil that can profit."

- John Galt, in Atlas Shrugged by Ayn Rand

A common critique of regenerative agriculture is that criticizing industrial agriculture is divisive and undermines the broader agricultural system. If this were true, meaningful change would be impossible. We live by stories and narratives, whether we recognize it or not. Any new technology will only be adopted if it aligns with the prevailing value structure—the implicit story we tell ourselves about how the world works.

Industrial agriculture and what society calls "regenerative agriculture" do not share the same foundation. They emerge from entirely different worldviews and are governed by opposing value structures. And in the long run, one will outcompete the other. There is no permanent compromise between these systems. The future of agriculture will not be a slightly modified industrial model—it will be a transformed, decentralized, ecologically integrated system that resolves the fundamental tensions between agriculture and nature. Traditionally, the conflict has been framed as cattle taking from the ecology. This is why we hear terms like "sustainable" or "responsible" ranching—language that suggests minimizing harm rather than maximizing ecological benefit. But when we recognize that large herbivores are not a burden on nature but a critical part of its operating system, the entire equation shifts. The fundamental conflict dissolves, and a clear path forward emerges.

Over time, systems that work against natural law unravel. Industrial agriculture, dependent on force, externalized costs, and continuous intervention, cannot persist indefinitely. But change does not mean reckless upheaval. The transition must be deliberate—avoiding unnecessary harm while decisively moving away from extractive, degenerative practices. A future of abundance and ecological integrity is not fantasy; it is a necessity. Feeding humanity and restoring the land are not opposing goals—they are inextricably linked.

But before we can build the right system, we must accept the right story. The narratives we adopt determine the world we create. And history has shown that the most compelling story—the one that best aligns with reality—is the one that endures.

Let us examine these two competing paradigms—one built on extraction and domination, the other on reciprocity and renewal. *The Story of Force* is one of control, compulsion, and short-term gains extracted at the expense of long-term viability. *The Story of Harmony*, by contrast, follows nature's logic, where cooperation and voluntary participation drive abundance. One of these stories will define the future.

THE STORY OF FORCE: BREAKING NATURE TO OUR WILL

The confinement, or feedlot, model is a compelling story. On the surface, it appears efficient, productive, and logical. It promises predictability, control, and high output. But beneath its carefully engineered façade, this system is fundamentally flawed—disconnected from the ecological realities that sustain it. At its core, *The Story of Force* seeks to dominate nature rather than work with it, enforcing unnatural constraints on a world that was never meant to be controlled.

The feedlot model is the endpoint of cheap fossil energy and the reductionist belief that cattle exist solely to produce protein for humans. It is an ecological, ethical, and even economic miscalculation of the highest order. When we remove cattle from the land, we strip them of their ecological function, forcing them into an artificial, resource-intensive system. In doing so, we do not improve efficiency; we externalize its costs—burying them in fossil fuel inputs, water depletion, topsoil loss, antibiotic reliance, and the slow unraveling of ecosystem health. Feedlots deliver highly predictable results, and in a civilization addicted to predictability, this is seen as a strength. But predictability in defiance of natural law is a fragile illusion. The entire industrial model rests on energy subsidies—fossil fuels, synthetic fertilizers, chemical pest control, and a global supply chain finely tuned to withstand only minor disruptions. This is a system that depends on constant intervention to suppress variability rather than harnessing it.

We have built a house of cards and convinced ourselves it is a fortress.

This illusion is only made possible by forcing a series of deeply unnatural circumstances:

- Cropland must be reduced to monoculture.
- Cattle must be removed from the land and confined in feedlots.
- Livestock must be fed unnatural diets in unnatural quantities.
- The entire system must be propped up with synthetic inputs to sustain the illusion of stability.

This is the height of forcing an outcome by repressing the voluntary, self-organizing imperatives of life. It is a story of life severed from its ecological function—a system propped up by energy and inputs that cannot last.

If we step back and examine this system within the larger framework of biological reality, we see it for what it truly is: a temporary workaround rather than a lasting solution. *The Story of Force* does not offer abundance—it merely delays collapse.

The question we must ask ourselves is this: Are we prepared to continue investing in an extractive system that requires ever greater interventions to stave off its own failure? Or is it time to embrace a model rooted in nature's logic—one that is self-sustaining rather than self-destructive?

Let us turn from force to harmony.

THE STORY OF HARMONY: RETURNING TO THE DANCE OF LIFE

The regenerative model will win the day in the long run—by definition. Any system that thrives over an infinite time horizon must be self-sustaining, self-repairing, and self-replicating. Only a system built on voluntary participation can achieve this. Nature does not sustain itself through force. It thrives through interaction, reciprocity, and renewal.

Regenerative ranchers do not force cattle to act against their nature. Instead, they align their management practices with the fundamental ecological drivers that have shaped grazing systems for millions of years.

The land is allowed to grow the plants it wants to grow. Cattle move to fresh grass of their own volition. The dung beetles work voluntarily. The cowbirds and cattle egrets voluntarily accompany the herd, picking off insects.

Nothing in this system is coerced. Everything functions through incentives rather than interventions.

Even the fencing used in regenerative systems—often

a single strand of electric wire—is not about force but guidance. This mimics the predator pressures that once governed large migratory herds, ensuring high-density grazing, even forage use, and adequate rest for the land. In a properly functioning ecology, staying grouped together is a voluntary survival strategy.

The regenerative story is one of perpetual creation. Rather than suppressing nature's rhythms, we learn to move with them—subtly guiding the system toward abundance rather than forcing it into submission. This is a story of humility rather than hubris, of participation rather than dominance.

When we align with the voluntary forces of nature, we create a system that does not require constant intervention. Instead of externalizing costs, we internalize benefits:

- Soil becomes deeper, richer, and more resilient.
- Water cycles become more efficient and self-replenishing.
- Biodiversity flourishes, naturally increasing stability and productivity.
- Cattle act as keystone species, cycling nutrients and regenerating landscapes.

This is a better story. It is the story of perpetual creation rather than forced extraction. It is the difference between standing against nature with a clenched fist or extending a hand in partnership.

The *Story of Harmony* is not about controlling nature—it is about becoming part of it.

THE CYCLES OF LIFE AND DEATH

"Guilt is what is wiped out by the myth. It is not a personal act; you are performing the world of nature."

- Joseph Campbell

"There, the hunt leaves no blood on my hands."

- Archie Roach

Trees are alive. Grass is alive. Rocks are alive. Everything we consider matter is alive and conscious. Could we even go so far as to say that even all the things we don't consider matter are alive? Magnetic fields? Ideas? We break ourselves off from the greatest part of creation when we reject the aliveness of mountains, streams, grains of sand, far-off galaxies, and particularly vivid daydreams. It is all the Great One doing somersaults. When we can recognize everything that we perceive as alive, we enter into communion with existence. Much of our suffering and our confusion comes from a deep rejection of the aliveness of the universe.

It is no wonder that a society raised in a terrarium of separateness struggles to tear off the roof, to let the sunlight touch the soil of our oneness. But once that roof is gone, the ideas in this book no longer need explanation; they simply are. They rise like the first green shoot through broken ground, self-evident and undeniable. Asking a culture built on separateness to open its heart to this understanding is no small thing. And yet, this is the work of the great adepts—Jesus, Buddha, and those unnamed mystics who have, since time immemorial, pointed toward the same shining reality. Awakening is the great undertaking of existence, and to step into its flow requires only that we turn toward it. The Book of Matthew says, "Ask, and it shall be given you; seek, and ye shall find; knock, and it shall be opened unto you."

When I experienced what Christian mystics might call a "visitation," it rewrote the architecture of my existence. What I once glimpsed in fragments, I now see as a whole. The world, which had seemed firm, real, and opaque, softened into a translucent infiniteness—somehow even more real. I could see the gears turning inside the machine, the bearings spinning in their housings—driving the great life of this magnificent mechanism. I could look at one piece, then the whole, and see that they were one and the same.

I don't claim this as some rare gift or singular revelation; I suspect it is simply what happens when we begin to truly see. Death, once the shadow that loomed over life, became part of its brilliance. I no longer dread its arrival. In some quiet way, I welcome it—not as an end, but as a turning, another step in the rhythm of existence. Once death loses its grip on us, we no longer fear it; we hold its power in our hands while alive and, when the time comes, gently offer ourselves to it.

We cannot take a step without wielding the power of life and death. We cannot even breathe without it. To live is to kill—this is not a moral failing but the structure of existence itself. To refuse to act for fear of causing death is to misunderstand life, for death denied does not disappear. It simply moves beyond our sight, twisting into strange, dishonorable forms, shaping the world in ways we refuse to see.

Take, for example, the belief that we must abandon animal agriculture and eat only that which lacks a face—things distant enough from us to preserve the illusion of their 'otherness.' But are fruits not the fertilized eggs of the tree? Does the tree not love its offspring as we love our own? And is it truly better to sterilize the living earth—erasing its wild complexity to plant endless rows of soy and corn—feeding a civilization that has dulled itself into thinking it can live without cost, while its own sickness quietly grows?

When we try to avoid all death, we do not spare life—we simply shift the burden of our energetic needs elsewhere. But what if embracing the cycle of life and death for herd animals could restore the prairies, savannas, and forests that once sustained them, rather than replacing their brilliant complexity with ordered rows of crops, each acre sterilized of the creatures that once called it home? What if the herds were so great and the ecology so rich that they could feed humanity on a scale now conventionally thought impossible? The answer is not to evade death, but to work toward the greatest abundance of life—and to honor the death that makes it so.

Here is an uncomfortably beautiful truth: the path to a world brimming with life begins with embracing our own death—not as an end, but as a promise of renewal. When we release our fear of death, we step into life fully. Even one person who does this thunders through the world like a herd unto himself, leaving life blooming in his wake.

There is a Blackfoot myth popularized by Joseph Campbell that speaks to the immortal relationship between man and buffalo:

> *Long ago, a Blackfoot tribe struggled to secure enough meat for the winter. Their usual method was to stampede bison over a cliff, but this year, it wasn't working. Each time they tried, the buffalo would veer away from the cliff's edge. The village grew anxious as the threat of famine loomed.*
>
> *One morning, a young girl from the tribe woke to do her chores. When she went to draw water, she spotted the buffalo herd standing near the cliff. In desperation, she cried out, "If only you would go over the cliff, I would marry one of you!"*
>
> *To her astonishment, the buffalo began leaping off the cliff. It was a miracle. But to her even greater shock, one of the buffalo approached her, ready to hold her to her promise. Honoring her word, as the buffalo had kept theirs, she left with him.*
>
> *When her family awoke and found her missing, they quickly discovered that she had run off with a buffalo. Her father, determined to find her, set off in search. After a time, he sat to rest at a buffalo wallow, where a magpie landed nearby. The father asked, "My daughter has gone off with a buffalo. Do you know where they are?"*
>
> *"Yes," replied the magpie, "they're not far from here."*

"Would you tell her that her father is waiting at the wallow?" the father asked.

The magpie flew off and delivered the message. The girl was immediately worried, sensing trouble. Begrudgingly, she told the magpie, "Tell him I'll be right there."

That morning, her buffalo husband awoke and handed her one of his horns. "Get me some water," he said.

"Okay," she replied, and made her way to the wallow.

When she arrived, her father grabbed her arm and whispered urgently, "We're going home."

"I can't," she said. "The herd will come after us." She filled the horn with water and returned to the herd.

But when she returned, her husband could smell her father's scent on her. She tried to deny it, but the buffalo wasn't fooled. Letting out a great bellow, he summoned the herd. They charged to the wallow and trampled her father into the ground.

Devastated by her father's death, the girl wept. Her buffalo husband said, "Why do you cry for him when so many of my brothers and sisters just died for you?"

Moved by compassion, the buffalo made an offer: "If you can bring your father back to life, I'll set you free."

The girl turned to the magpie and asked for help

> *in finding a piece of her father's body. Eventually, the magpie found a small piece of vertebrae. The girl placed it under her blanket and sang a sacred reviving song. When she lifted the blanket, her father appeared, though he wasn't alive yet. She sang a little longer, and her father stood up, fully revived.*
>
> *The buffalo were amazed and asked, "Can you do this for us? We'll teach you the buffalo dance so that when you kill our families, you can use it to bring us back to life.'"*

Each year, as the buffalo were hunted, the Blackfoot would perform the Buffalo Dance, a ceremony that did not merely honor the animals but ensured their return. This ritual was not just tradition; it was an act of participation in the eternal cycle—a means of absolving the creeping, paralyzing guilt that arises when a culture grows too distant from nature.

It is the killing that brings the buffalo back to life. It is the death of the old members of the tribe that keeps the tribe alive. It is the interplay between them that keeps them both alive. As a tree must age, die, fall, and fertilize the forest floor, we must all die to fertilize the future. Additionally, this story points to the constant revivifying interplay between the world of conscious awareness, the material plane, and the dimension "behind" it. The dimension behind it is, of course, the great empty field from which all things arise—which is, in fact, none other than our very existence here and now.

In the story, we can read the magpie as the intermediary between these realms. He is the shaman, the messenger between worlds—the connective tissue binding dimensions together. He carries knowledge between the seen and the unseen, the conscious and the unconscious. The marriage between the girl and the buffalo is not just a union of two beings but a reflection of the indivisibility of humans and the animal world. They are joined not only by ceremony but by the inescapable reality of the cycle itself: all things are called forth from the void, and all things return to it.

The girl's blanket is death. It is under the blanket of death that the revivification takes place. The body of the father who was trampled and the body of the father who stood up again are the same. It is thus with the buffalo. It is thus with us. Our grandchildren are our very body. Children born a thousand years from now on Mars will be our body. Mars itself is our body now. This has, in the final analysis, no limits—between individuals, between species, between planets, between time itself. All life—all existence—is one body, and the death of one "individual" is nothing but the formation and dissolution of a single cell in an organism too vast to name.

When cultures live and die within temporary, artificial luxury—insulated from the respiration of nature—we forget how to breathe with the world. It is as if we are holding our breath, trapped in a pause that cannot last. To sever ourselves from the natural cycles is to sever ourselves from death, and in doing so, we sever ourselves from life itself. We lose the knowing—not an intellectual understanding, but a deep, visceral knowing—that life and death are not separate forces but one continuous motion.

Our individual cells rise and fall, just as the tides, just

as the stars, just as the herds that move across the land. Our entire existence is an ebb and flow of formation and dissolution within the one great ocean of being. We are but an island of flesh in an endless sea of grass—rising, falling, blinking in, blinking out.

This rhythm holds true in the relationship between graziers and cattle. The dance has not ended; only its setting has changed. We take the place of the predators, the cattle take the place of the herds, and together we reenact the eternal play. We kill, and in killing, we give life. This is what my grandfather meant when he said, "There's no retirement in ranching." There is no opting out of the buffalo dance. The predator is in our own backyard. The tiger is you and me.

A grazier, if he does his work well, spends himself in service of the whole. This is the mission of every living thing. To step fully into this reality is to be freed of the illusion of control, to be unburdened by the guilt of participation. The work remains, but suffering falls away. When we accept our place in the cycle—when we know it in our bones—we are no longer trapped in the fear of death. We move as the herds move, we die as the trees die, and we return, again and again, to life.

AWAKENING TO RESPONSIBILITY

It is unlikely that Indigenous Americans obsessed over the marbling or tenderness of buffalo meat. No doubt they recognized that animals were fattest at the end of the rainy season and leaner in times of drought, but they did not attempt to engineer nature to produce a standardized steak. Their relationship with the land was not one of command but of collaboration.

To say they left the land untouched would be an oversimplification. They set fire to grasslands to renew them, devised ingenious hunting methods, and cultivated crops—but they did not demand that nature conform to their whims. Their relationship with the land was one of conversation, not control. Unlike modern agriculture, which bends landscapes into strict and unwavering obedience, Indigenous cultures worked within the natural rhythms of their world. Many likely could not even conceive of the rigid separation from nature that defines much of modern life, the unspoken assumption that humanity stands apart from the land rather than within it.

The Western and Eastern traditions diverge in their fundamental relationship with nature. In much of the Western world, nature is perceived as fallen, something to be tamed, corrected, and redeemed. This assumption—perhaps the most dangerous of our civilization—sets the stage for endless conflict between humans and the land. In contrast, Eastern traditions do not frame nature as broken. It simply is. It gives and it takes, destroys and renews, not as a thing apart, but as something we are inextricably woven into. We cannot degrade nature without degrading ourselves, just as we cannot restore nature without restoring some part of our own being.

Reality is a field of mysteries—some of which can be observed, analyzed, and enhanced—and some of which we may never approach conceptually or intuitively. It is, after all, an endlessly deep abyss that will never be fully sounded or mapped, but from which an endless supply of miracles and experiences can be meted out. If we can accept this, we might meet existence with greater humility and openness. This is the wisdom of the Wright Flyer—let us accept and learn to love the uncertainty of the breeze, and we will enjoy gliding across it all the more.

Though Western civilization has grown less overtly Christian, its foundation remains deeply so. The threads of Christian theology are woven through even our secular structures, shaping our collective understanding of labor, suffering, and redemption. The Western tradition stands atop a singular moment in Genesis—the moment where consciousness was met with consequence:

> *"And to Adam He said:*
>
> *'Because you have listened to the voice of your wife*
>
> *and have eaten from the tree*
>
> *of which I commanded you not to eat,*
>
> *cursed is the ground because of you;*
>
> *through toil you will eat of it*
>
> *all the days of your life.*
>
> *Both thorns and thistles it will yield for you,*

and you will eat the plants of the field.

By the sweat of your brow

you will eat your bread.'" – Genesis 3:17-19

In other words: With knowledge comes toil. The moment we became aware of our own mortality, we became bound to struggle, forced to wrest sustenance from an earth that no longer offers it freely. Survival is no longer granted; it must be earned.

There is a quiet tension within the regenerative movement, embedded in the very word *regenerative*. It carries the whisper of return—of resurrecting a lost world. Perhaps this is not the explicit goal of those who have thought deeply about it, but words are vessels, and meaning drifts on unseen currents. Even the best sailors are sometimes carried where they did not intend to go.

Western civilization holds an unspoken belief that we were exiled from the Garden and that our work is to find our way back. It is right to long for a world in balance, to want the land to thrive beneath our hands. But there is no road back—only forward. Any return to abundance will not be a restoration of what was, but the conscious creation of something new. The Garden of Eden, the Pleistocene, the lost landscapes of plenty—these were not times of perfect design but times when we existed in unconscious or semi-conscious union with the land. Let us not chase a fading mirage. Let us build a world even more abundant than the one we lost.

Imagine a great wooden lodge, high in the mountains, its beams hewn from the towering trees of a forest long vanished. The lodge still stands, but its timbers groan with age, its walls surrendering to time. Those who live within dream of restoring it to its original form, but the tools that built it are lost, and the trees that bore it are gone. They cannot rebuild it as it was. But they *can* build something new—something stronger, more enduring. And as they build, a new forest rises around them, one that will outlive them, shading the generations to come.

The word *regenerative* carries a promise of life renewed, and its rise in our lexicon marks a shift in the right direction. But all sharp knives dull with use. Language, like the land, must be tended. It must be tested against reality, refined against the whetstone of experience.

In my boldest vision, I see Earth as an optimized grazing system. To some, this may sound sacrilegious, particularly within the modern conservationist fold. But as I have shown, our planet—at least during the Pleistocene—was already a semi-optimized grazing system. Grasslands and their attendant species did not emerge in a vacuum; they co-evolved with vast herds of herbivores and the predators that shaped them. It is not only appropriate but necessary to view most landscapes through a grazing lens. Predators cycle herbivores. Herbivores cycle forage. Forage captures sunlight. We all exist to feed each other.

Joseph Campbell said it simply:

"Life is just a game of, 'now you eat me'!"

Some argue that increasing domesticated herbivore populations has come at the expense of wild creatures. But any skilled grazier knows that improving landscape function does not diminish wildlife—it invites it back. Healthier landscapes support more life, not less. Predators cycle herbivores, and without their presence—whether in the form of wolves, lions, or the hand of the grazier—the system atrophies.

The sharp teeth of the wolf, the lion's claws, the hawk's talons—these were nature's first architects. Today, we inherit that role. We are predators still, but evolved ones—predators who understand not only the needs of the hunt but the needs of the whole. It is no longer enough to kill and consume; we must move with the wisdom of the land itself, ensuring that life flourishes in the wake of death.

The Genesis text suggests that Adam and Eve, upon eating the apple, became fundamentally different—separated from the living world in a way no other creature had been. Once, nature had sustained them freely, their survival embedded in the rhythms of the land. But with consciousness came distance, and with distance came toil. Spiritually and ecologically severed from their original state, they could no longer exist within nature's abundance. They had to extract what they needed from a world that no longer gave freely.

Thus, agriculture arose—not as the next step in an inevitable march toward progress, but as a survival mechanism. It was not a linear evolution of human greatness, but a workaround for a world that had ceased to provide. The land no longer offered itself up as home, so humanity, blessed with an oversized brain and desperate ingenuity, carved out its own. The act of planting seeds and harvesting grain may have begun as a small, practical innovation, but as with so many human endeavors, what was once a simple adaptation became an all-consuming force. In just a few hundred generations, we have allowed our tether to our Pleistocene homeland to fray. In its place, we have built a system that prizes immediate caloric abundance over the deeper, more enduring wealth of a thriving ecology.

For most of human history, our presence on the land was small enough that nature could absorb our excesses. If we over-extracted from one place, we simply moved on, and the land healed in our absence. Even as recently as my father's youth in the Iowa cornfields, farmers still left a few unharvested rows for the deer—a faint echo of the ancient reciprocity that once bound people to the land. But such gestures, however well-intentioned, did little to offset the immense, unseen toll of industrial farming. With every tilling and every harvest, countless small creatures met their end beneath the machinery of progress.

Today, with humanity nearing 8 billion, even those small gestures have disappeared. Few farmers leave anything behind for the handful of wild beings that remain. Our relationship with the land has shifted from unthinking excess to outright extraction, and the language of stewardship has become little more than a veil over systematic exploitation. The cycle of life and death still governs the world, but we have ceased to acknowledge it. Instead of honoring the cost of our survival, we have done our best to hide it. But hiding does not absolve us of responsibility. If anything, it makes the reckoning more urgent. We must take a hard look at what we have built from this explosion of resource consumption and turn our ingenuity toward something greater: not just sustaining ourselves, but creating a world where life flourishes in the wake of our presence, not in spite of it.

We began as creatures moving through the world in a state of unconscious harmony, acting not by choice but by instinct. Then, in the long unfolding of history, we awoke—to ourselves, to our own mortality, to the knowledge that we could shape the world rather than simply move within it. Animals do not need conscious principles to guide them; their way is woven seamlessly into the fabric of existence. But we, in stepping beyond instinct, inherited both power and peril. Our ability to manipulate the environment means that we are uniquely capable of catastrophe—but also uniquely capable of creation. It is precisely because we can shape the world that we must do so with wisdom.

The human race is the most powerful force in the history of creation. And with that power comes responsibility—not just to prevent destruction, but to envision something greater. We must pull from the depths of our dreaming an image of outrageous beauty and bring it forth into reality. It is our destiny, not to recoil from the world, but to set our hands to the work of its renewal—to take all that we are, all that we have learned, and build something that sings with life.

EPILOGUE
A NEW EDEN

"Arrakis could be an Eden if its rulers would look up from grubbing for spice!"

-Liet Kynes, Dune

Planet Earth requires a herd-driven ecological reawakening to reverse the accelerating decline of its habitats. But this cannot be a simple multiplication of herd animals, left to roam as they once did. The world they evolved in no longer exists as it did. Our landscapes are now defined by highways, industrial corridors, sprawling cities, and meticulously cultivated farmland. The ancient migrations that once sustained entire ecosystems stretched for thousands of miles, but such unfettered movement is no longer possible in a world criss-crossed with human infrastructure. Instead, we must create a new form of migration—one that mimics the impact of these lost patterns within the constraints of our modern reality.

This means that across thousands of farms, ranches, wildlife preserves, and public lands, well-managed herds of genetically adapted animals must be reintroduced at high densities, functioning as keystone actors in their respective ecosystems. This will not happen by chance. It requires a deliberate, large-scale investment in fencing, water infrastructure, and land management—a foundational reinvestment in the very circulatory system of our landscapes.

This investment must be deliberate and strategic. Land managers would be wise to develop long-term plans—spanning 5, 10, 25, 50, and even 100 years—outlining a clear trajectory for landscape regeneration. These plans should prioritize two core pillars: infrastructure and herd genetics. Beyond these, considerations such as ecological succession, community involvement, and the development of ecosystem services must be integrated. The specifics will vary by region, but the underlying principle remains: success depends on forward-thinking design and commitment.

At the heart of these plans lies a single objective—establishing a clear timeline and financial strategy for building out water distribution and fencing infrastructure in a way that maximizes sustainable stocking rates. Stocking rate is not arbitrary; it is dictated by two critical variables: the amount of forage produced and the percentage of that forage effectively harvested. Raising stocking rates within ecological limits is not just an economic necessity—it is the most powerful tool available for improving soil health, increasing biodiversity, and ensuring long-term profitability through the intelligent application of herd effect.

Most ranches today operate on razor-thin profit margins, with their financial viability largely dictated by the industrial beef supply chain. This presents an inherent contradiction: the cattle that maximize profits for the feedlot and slaughterhouse are not the same cattle that maximize profitability or ecological function for the rancher. Industrial processors favor large-framed animals that perform well in a confined setting, yet these same animals require excessive inputs in a pasture-based system. The cattle best suited for regenerative grazing—smaller-framed, denser animals that thrive on grass alone—are often penalized in the current system. One of the defining challenges of the next century in ranching is resolving this conflict: how can ranchers transition toward ecologically adapted cattle while ensuring that their profitability is not undercut by an industry designed to reward a different kind of animal?

This is not a condemnation of meatpackers. My critique is systemic, not personal. People respond to incentives, and the modern beef supply chain has been structured to maximize efficiency within the context of fossil-fuel-driven, extractive agriculture. This model makes economic sense in the short term, but it is eroding our landscapes and placing long-term food security at risk. My argument throughout this book has been simple: aligning our agricultural practices with natural systems is not just an ecological necessity—it is an economic imperative. By making a few key shifts, we can create a system that rewards the kind of management that builds soil, restores biodiversity, and ensures a future for ranching itself.

In light of this reality, I am proposing the equivalent of a "Manhattan Project" for high-density grazing. The original Manhattan Project was a wartime initiative that funneled vast resources into the development of a weapon capable of altering the course of history. Imagine if we applied that same level of urgency and investment toward life rather than destruction—toward building ecological abundance instead of unraveling it. Two billion dollars were spent in 1940 to bring forth the atomic bomb; in today's terms, that's roughly $45 billion. That sum would go a long way in reshaping American agriculture toward a model that regenerates landscapes, increases food security, and creates economic resilience for those who tend the land.

This is not a naïve call for unchecked government spending. I recognize the dangers of bureaucracy, inefficiency, and unintended consequences. But the scale of the problem demands bold solutions, and history has shown that when we decide something is a priority, we find a way. The question is not whether we can afford to invest in rebuilding our ecological foundation—it's whether we can afford not to.

INFRASTRUCTURE FOR A LIVING LANDSCAPE

A project of this scale would require strategic investment, possibly through a mix of government-backed grants, market-driven incentives, and innovative financial instruments such as "grazing bonds"—structured funding mechanisms dedicated to ecosystem restoration through optimized herd activity. These programs could function at federal, state, or even private levels, with philanthropic organizations playing a key role in bridging the gaps where government funding falls short.

Critics may argue that such programs would disproportionately benefit large landowners, but the ecological imperative outweighs ideological quibbles. Restoring herd-driven landscape function is not a luxury; it is a necessity. While distribution of benefits must be carefully structured to avoid reinforcing existing inequities, the reality is that large-scale landowners steward vast portions of the world's grazable land. The return of properly managed herbivory across these landscapes is too vital to be derailed by concerns that, while worth addressing, should not take precedence over action. Additionally, such financial instruments need not be confined solely to grazing—similar models could be adapted to fund a range of ecosystem optimization projects, from reforestation initiatives to soil carbon sequestration programs.

Organizations involved in conservation easements could integrate infrastructure investment into their development rights agreements, allocating funds specifically for fencing and water improvements. This approach ensures that land designated for conservation is also set up for productive, ecologically beneficial grazing rather than being left as static, underutilized acreage.

Crucially, these investments need not be exorbitant. Far too much money has been spent erecting unnecessary 4- or 5-strand barbed wire cross-fences when a single line of electrified high-tensile wire is not only more effective but also cheaper, easier to manage, and more wildlife-friendly. On well-managed ranches where cattle are accustomed to frequent movement and high-density grazing, a single hot wire is all that's needed. I've seen my own cattle push right through a conventional barbed-wire fence while showing complete respect for a single strand of electrified polywire.

Of course, perhaps fencing itself will soon become obsolete. The rapid advancement of drone and virtual fencing technologies—AI-driven collars, autonomous shepherd drones—suggests that within a few decades, we may no longer be physically containing animals at all. Maybe the future sounds less like a crackling electric fence and more like Doc Brown from *Back to the Future Part II*: "Fences? Where we're going, we don't need fences!"

HERDS OF THE FUTURE: ADAPTED GENETICS

Following the foundational principles laid out in this book, all genetic selection for cattle operations should be guided by a singular focus: maximizing fertility with minimal inputs. Any fixation on individual traits—be it frame size, coat color, or carcass characteristics—misses the point entirely. Fertility is the ultimate expression of ecological and biological fitness, the point where all valuable traits converge. If we select for animals that thrive and reproduce efficiently in a truly naturalized grazing system, we set ourselves up for long-term ecological and economic success.

Yet, the cattle industry still clings to arbitrary and, at times, counterproductive aesthetic preferences. American, Canadian, and Southern Australian markets favor black cattle. Colombian and Northern Australian markets prefer white. South African markets lean toward red. Anything outside of these arbitrary preferences is discounted. This fixation on color—as if the hue of a hide has any bearing on ecological performance—belongs in the dustbin of history. The only meaningful measure of an animal's worth should be its ability to thrive within the context of its land. Over time, we will find that the cattle most suited to a truly pasture-based system are precisely those the commercial industry has spent decades overlooking. Why? Because industrial efficiency and ecological efficiency are not the same thing—and in many ways, they are in direct opposition.

No two ranches are alike. Even neighboring operations, divided only by a fence, exist under different forces—variations in soil, water availability, herd genetics, and management philosophy. The land itself speaks through the cattle that graze it. But that voice is muffled when herds are propped up by prophylactic anthelmintics, high-energy supplements, and constant preferential grazing. Under such conditions, it is not the voice of the land that speaks—it is the voice of resource extraction.

The feedlot system's obsession with "efficiency" forces cow-calf producers into a role they were never meant to play: subsidizing the profitability of downstream processors at the expense of their own land's health. The illusion of efficiency is maintained through preferential grazing—a short-term gain that exploits soil fertility and weakens ecosystem resilience. The irony is that true efficiency—the kind that maximizes fertility, reduces inputs, and builds soil—has been ignored for generations in favor of artificial gains that come at a long-term cost.

Take anthelmintics (dewormers), for example. They are a direct exploitation of fossil energy-enabled fertility, and their ecological consequences ripple through the system. Dewormers don't just target parasites; they decimate dung beetle populations, disrupting a critical component of soil health. High-energy feed supplements, too, are an extractive practice—shuffling fertility from one landscape to another, always at the cost of fossil fuel inputs. These interventions do not add to the system; they deplete it, delaying the inevitable reckoning that all extractive models eventually face.

Any organization backing this "Manhattan Project" should enshrine ecologically sound selection criteria in its governing documents. The goal must be to maximize fertility in high-density grazing regimes, not chase artificial production traits that undermine ecological function. For those looking to refine their understanding of this process, I direct you back to *Man, Cattle, and Veld* by Johann Zietsman—a masterful exploration of selecting cattle for true efficiency.

DECENTRALIZING ABBATOIRS: THE KEY TO LOCAL HARMONY

The industrial beef system contains an internal contradiction that makes it fundamentally incompatible with the ecological role of cattle. As discussed in the section on Feed Conversion Efficiency, the structure of the slaughter industry prioritizes uniformity and scale over ecological function. If you were a slaughterhouse owner, your business would depend on maximizing throughput—processing as much beef per unit of time, labor, and energy as possible. This goal is best served by highly standardized carcasses, which is why feedlots produce animals tailored for industrial predictability rather than regenerative resilience.[39]

This system does not harmonize with the infinite variation of the natural world. It is a machine designed to process uniformity, but nature does not produce uniformity. Future advances in robotics and artificial intelligence may one day bridge this gap, reducing the inefficiencies caused by varied carcass sizes. But waiting for future technology to solve our present misalignment is not a plan. Instead, we should invest in decentralization—establishing a network of small-to-medium-sized slaughter facilities, each scaled to process a manageable number of cattle per day while adapting to regional needs and ecological conditions. These facilities would be more adaptable to the realities of regenerative operations and could be independently powered by solar, hydrogen, or integrated into nuclear-driven microgrids.

I do not claim to have every answer to the financial, political, and logistical questions that such a vision would raise. But I do know this: the ecology and the economy are radically out of step with each other, and that discord is driving us toward collapse. I have faith that as we move with clear intention toward a better world, the right people will appear, bringing the expertise and resolve needed to solve the problems ahead. What follows is not a rigid blueprint, but a glimpse—a possible future if we choose to align ourselves with nature rather than against it.

---

39. Hennessy, D.A. (2005), Slaughterhouse Rules: Animal Uniformity and Regulating for Food Safety in Meat Packing. American Journal of Agricultural Economics, 87: 600-609. https://doi.org/10.1111/j.1467-8276.2005.00750.x

IMAGINING THE NEW EDEN

You awaken to the quiet hum of a world in balance.

It is the year 2149. The first rays of morning light slip through the drapes, catching dust motes as they drift in slow spirals. You swing your legs over the side of the bed, careful not to wake your spouse. The night was undisturbed—no alarms, no urgent calls for intervention. The land, the systems, the herds—all are functioning as they should. Grazing drones, autonomous mowers, a solar-powered microgrid, and a carefully managed water system keep the landscape alive and thriving, allowing you the rarest luxury of all: deep, untroubled sleep.

Your tea is already brewed, steam curling in the morning air as you settle into the quiet rhythm of the day. You take a slow sip, letting its warmth stir you fully awake, then open your journal to jot down a few lines—reflections, gratitude, a note about the work ahead.

"Heidi, how's the land today?"

Your AI pastoral assistant responds in her measured voice, detailing the state of the grazing rotation, water levels, and herd behavior. There is nothing out of order—just the slow, steady pulse of a landscape functioning as it should. Your spouse and children gather around the breakfast table, and you discuss the day's plans—not with urgency, but with the easy confidence of people living in alignment with their world.

After breakfast, you step outside, the air crisp and charged with the scent of earth. Your transport glides silently across the land, carrying you toward the herd. The cattle are bunched tightly, their heads down in thick, knee-high grass—lush in a way that would have been unthinkable in the 2020s.

Above them, the grazing drones—your mechanical "sheepdogs"—hover with quiet precision, guiding the herd to fresh pasture as soon as they've finished their allotment. There was a time when cattle needed constant intervention—dewormers, supplemental feed, careful monitoring through the bitter winter months. But after generations of selection for fertility and hardiness, these animals now thrive on their own, tuned to the rhythm of the land. Even the climate has softened in response to the restored landscape. Winters no longer bite so deep, summers no longer burn so hot. The land, the animals, and the seasons are moving in concert again.

By 2149, the planet hums with life. Most of Earth's landscapes have returned to a state of breathtaking ecological function—grasslands rich with movement, savannas dappled with light and shadow, forests no longer choked by stagnation but opened up by the hooves of moving herds. The careful reintroduction of high-density grazing has transformed once-declining ecosystems. The overgrown, fire-prone woodlands have given way to a dynamic balance—grasses and forbs thriving beneath scattered trees, creating a mosaic of habitats teeming with biodiversity.

Even the prairies, long thought to be at the mercy of soil depletion, have reclaimed their former abundance. Trees and shrubs have woven themselves back into the landscape, not as invaders but as returning neighbors. With the land's revival, evolution has quickened its pace. New species have emerged—life finding unexpected niches in the renewed complexity. In place of the simplified, human-imposed ecosystems of centuries past, the Earth now carries a greater harmony than perhaps ever before.

Over the next century, global population dynamics shifted. After peaking at 9 billion, humanity gradually settled into a more balanced presence, now numbering closer to 5 billion. But the greatest shift was not in our numbers—it was in our reach. Several million now live on Mars, where the first cattle grazed inside atmospheric domes in 2047. In this, Mother Earth had achieved her great goal—her own reproduction. Life, once bound to a single world, had seeded itself among the stars. What was once unthinkable had become inevitable: Earth had given birth to new ecologies beyond herself, expanding the rhythms of life into places that had never known them.

Decentralized energy networks unlocked new ways of living, fueling a renaissance of rural life. With microgrids eliminating reliance on fragile, centralized power systems, half of humanity now lives on the land, actively managing ecosystems with the wisdom of centuries past and the technology of the present. Even those in the cities remain deeply engaged in the global ecology, understanding their role in the great exchange of life, energy, and renewal.

Humanity has fully stepped into its role—not as a conqueror of landscapes, but as a guardian of life's cycles, a shepherd of abundance. With the weight of unnecessary toil lifted, time itself feels different. The days are no longer measured in commutes and deadlines but in the rhythm of the land. The great distraction of industrial existence—spending hours each day in self-driven vehicles to perform tasks disconnected from our deeper human purpose—has faded into history. It is almost hard to believe we once lived that way.

We have returned to the Savanna, not in exile, but in triumph. This is not regression; it is the next turning of the wheel, the next iteration of humanity. We have relearned what was forgotten—that the path to prosperity lies in partnership with nature, not its subjugation. From the soil to the stars, we have stitched together what was once broken, and the result is a world alive with movement, color, and song. The great flowering of life has rarely been fuller, deeper, or richer.

This is the golden age—not of industry, not of empire, but of life itself. A time when humanity, at last, moves in step with the rhythm of the world, not against it. When the land flourishes beneath our care, when the sky is no longer something we conquer but something we expand into, carrying Earth's legacy beyond herself.

I'll see you there.

www.ingramcontent.com/pod-product-compliance
Lightning Source LLC
LaVergne TN
LVHW091324150826
845673LV00006B/1761

9798995291909